Congressional
Research
Service

China/Taiwan: Evolution of the "One China" Policy—Key Statements from Washington, Beijing, and Taipei

Shirley A. Kan

Specialist in Asian Security Affairs

June 24, 2011

Congressional Research Service

7-5700

www.crs.gov

RL30341

CRS Report for Congress ————————————————

Prepared for Members and Committees of Congress

Summary

Despite apparently consistent statements in four decades, the U.S. "one China" policy concerning Taiwan remains somewhat ambiguous and subject to different interpretations. Apart from questions about what the "one China" policy entails, issues have arisen about whether U.S. Presidents have stated clear positions and have changed or should change policy, affecting U.S. interests in security and democracy. In Part I, this CRS Report, updated as warranted, discusses the "one China" policy since the United States began in 1971 to reach presidential understandings with the People's Republic of China (PRC) government in Beijing. Part II records the evolution of policy as affected by legislation and key statements by Washington, Beijing, and Taipei. Taiwan formally calls itself the Republic of China (ROC), celebrating in 2011 the 100th anniversary of its founding. Policy covers three major issue areas: sovereignty over Taiwan; PRC use of force or coercion against Taiwan; and cross-strait dialogue. The United States recognized the ROC until the end of 1978 and has maintained an official, non-diplomatic relationship with Taiwan after recognition of the PRC in 1979. The United States did not explicitly state the sovereign status of Taiwan in the U.S.-PRC Joint Communiques of 1972, 1979, and 1982. The United States "acknowledged" the "one China" position of both sides of the Taiwan Strait.

Since 1971, U.S. Presidents—both secretly and publicly—have articulated a "one China" *policy* in understandings with the PRC. Congressional oversight has watched for any new agreements and any shift in the U.S. stance closer to that of Beijing's "one China" *principle*—on questions of sovereignty, arms sales, or dialogue. Not recognizing the PRC's claim over Taiwan or Taiwan as a sovereign state, U.S. policy has considered Taiwan's status as unsettled. With added conditions, U.S. policy leaves the Taiwan question to be resolved by the people on both sides of the strait: a "peaceful resolution" with the assent of Taiwan's people and without unilateral changes. In short, U.S. policy focuses on the *process* of resolution of the Taiwan question, not any set outcome.

The Taiwan Relations Act (TRA) of 1979, **P.L. 96-8**, has governed U.S. policy in the absence of a diplomatic relationship or a defense treaty. The TRA stipulates the expectation that the future of Taiwan "will be determined" by peaceful means. The TRA specifies that it is U.S. policy, among the stipulations: to consider any non-peaceful means to determine Taiwan's future "a threat" to the peace and security of the Western Pacific and of "grave concern" to the United States; "to provide Taiwan with arms of a defensive character;" and "to maintain the capacity of the United States to resist any resort to force or other forms of coercion" jeopardizing the security, or social or economic system of Taiwan's people. The TRA provides a congressional role in determining security assistance "necessary to enable Taiwan to maintain a sufficient self-defense capability." President Reagan also offered "Six Assurances" to Taipei in 1982, partly covering arms sales.

Policymakers have continued to face unresolved issues, while the political and strategic context of the policy has changed dramatically since the 1970s. Since the mid-1990s, U.S. interests in the military balance as well as peace and stability in the Taiwan Strait have been challenged by the PRC's military buildup (particularly in missiles) and coercion, resistance in Taiwan by the Kuomintang (KMT) party to raising defense spending, and moves perceived by Beijing for *de jure* independence under Democratic Progressive Party (DPP) President Chen Shui-bian (2000-2008). After May 2008, KMT President Ma Ying-jeou resumed the cross-strait dialogue (after a decade)—beyond seeking detente. With President Obama since 2009, a rhetorical convergence emerged among the three sides about "peaceful development" of cross-strait engagement, but disagreement has remained about the PRC's opposition to U.S. arms sales for Taiwan's defense. On June 16, 2011, the House Foreign Affairs Committee held a hearing: "Why Taiwan Matters."

Contents

Tables

Contacts

Part I: U.S. Policy on "One China"

Congressional Concerns

Paying particular attention to congressional influence on policy, this CRS Report discusses the U.S. "one China" *policy* concerning Taiwan since the United States (under the Nixon Administration) began in 1971 to reach understandings with the People's Republic of China (PRC) government, which has insisted on its "one China" *principle*. Based on open sources and interviews, this report also reviews comprehensively the evolution of the "one China" issue, as it has been articulated in key statements by Washington, Beijing, and Taipei.

In the 1990s, Congress pushed for **changes** in policy toward Taiwan. Questions about the "one China" policy arose again after Lee Teng-hui, President of Taiwan (formally called the Republic of China (ROC)), characterized cross-strait relations as "special state-to-state ties" on July 9, 1999. Beijing responded vehemently with calls for Lee to retract the perceived deviation from the "one China" position and reiterated long-standing threats to use force if necessary to prevent a declaration of independence by Taiwan. The PRC also questioned U.S. commitment to "one China" and expressed opposition to any U.S. military intervention. The Clinton Administration responded that Lee's statement was not helpful and reaffirmed the "one China" policy.[1] Some questioned whether U.S. law, the Taiwan Relations Act (TRA), P.L. 96-8, requires U.S. defense of Taiwan against an attack from the People's Liberation Army (PLA), China's military.

Senator Jesse Helms, Chairman of the Foreign Relations Committee, at a July 21, 1999 hearing, said that Lee "created an opportunity to break free from the anachronistic, Beijing-inspired one-China policy which has imprisoned U.S. policy toward China and Taiwan for years." Representative Benjamin Gilman, Chairman of the International Relations Committee, wrote in a September 7, 1999 letter to Clinton that it is a "common misperception" that we conceded officially that Beijing is the capital of the "one China" that includes Taiwan. He wrote, "under no circumstances should the United States move toward Beijing's version of 'one China'."[2]

Since 2001, U.S. policymakers have tended to stress **continuity** in maintaining the "one China" policy. During the George W. Bush Administration, leaders of the House and Senate stressed support for Taiwan as a democracy, rather than its independent status. Moreover, Members voiced concerns about cross-strait tension arising from actions taken by both Beijing and Taipei.

Senator Richard Lugar, Chairman of the Foreign Relations Committee, wrote in May 2001 that "for many years, successive U.S. administrations have affirmed that there is one China and that the people on Taiwan and the people of China should work out a plan for peaceful unification." He also referred to a debate on the nature of the U.S. obligation to "defend democracy in Taiwan" and to prevent a "forceful military unification of Taiwan and China."[3] Representative Henry Hyde, Chairman of the International Relations Committee, spoke in Beijing in December 2002

---

[1] Department of State, Press Briefing by James Rubin, July 15, 1999; Secretary of State Madeleine Albright's remarks on visit of Israeli Prime Minister Ehud Barak, July 20, 1999.

[2] Dalrymple, Mary, "Taiwanese President's Comment Inspires GOP to Renew Attack on Clinton's 'One China' Policy," *Congressional Quarterly*, July 24, 1999; Letter from Representative Benjamin Gilman to President Clinton, September 7, 1999.

[3] Richard Lugar, "Timely Exit for Ambiguity," *Washington Times*, May 17, 2001.

and dismissed notions that U.S. support for Taiwan is geared toward containing or dividing China. He said that "the bedrock of the very strong support for Taiwan in the U.S. Congress" is the shared experience as democracies. Moreover, Hyde highlighted Taiwan's significance as a model of a "Chinese democracy" that proved democracy is compatible with Chinese culture.[4]

As a focal point in the House for attention on Taiwan, an initial number of 85 Members formed a bipartisan Taiwan Caucus on April 9, 2002, with Representatives Robert Wexler, Steve Chabot, Sherrod Brown, and Dana Rohrabacher as co-chairs. Later, 10 Senators were original members of another Taiwan Caucus formed on September 17, 2003, with Senators George Allen and Tim Johnson as co-chairs. At two events at the Heritage Foundation in 2003 and 2004, Representatives Robert Andrews and Steve Chabot spoke critically of the "one China" policy.[5]

U.S. views were shaped by developments in Taiwan and concern about cross-strait tension. On August 3, 2002, President Chen Shui-bian of the Democratic Progressive Party (DPP) gave a speech using the phrase "one country on each side" of the strait, surprising Washington, even before the first anniversary of the September 11, 2001, terrorist attacks. Leading up to the presidential election on March 20, 2004, Chen advocated holding the first referendums (on the same day as the election) and drafting a new constitution with a timetable (new draft constitution by September 28, 2006; a referendum on the constitution on December 10, 2006; and enactment of the new constitution on May 20, 2008). Though symbolic steps, Beijing reacted with alarm.

On November 18, 2003, a PRC official on Taiwan affairs who is a PLA major general issued a threat to use force against what Beijing perceives as the "open promotion of Taiwan independence."[6] Deputy Secretary of State Richard Armitage responded by saying that "there's an election and campaign going on in Taiwan, and I think one shouldn't over-emphasize comments that are made in the heat of an election" and that the United States "has full faith that the question of Taiwan will be resolved peacefully." He added that the TRA guides policy in providing Taiwan "sufficient defense articles for her self-defense" and "also requires the United States to keep sufficient force in the Asia Pacific area to be able to keep the area calm." Armitage reaffirmed that the U.S. commitment to assist Taiwan's self-defense, with no defense treaty, "doesn't go beyond that in the Taiwan Relations Act, and we have good, competent military forces there."[7]

On the eve of his visit to Washington, PRC Premier Wen Jiabao warned on November 22, 2003, that China would "pay any price to safeguard the unity of the motherland."[8] On November 29, President Chen surprisingly announced that he would use one provision in the referendum law passed by the opposition-dominated legislature two days earlier and hold a "defensive referendum" on China's threats on the day of the presidential election. During his meeting with Premier Wen in the Oval Office on December 9, 2003, President Bush stated that he opposed Chen's efforts to change the status quo, drawing criticisms that Bush sided with the PRC's belligerence. The four co-chairmen of the Taiwan Caucus in the House wrote a letter to President

---

[4] Henry Hyde, "Remarks at Tsinghua University," Beijing, December 10, 2002.

[5] "Two Congressmen Look at 'One China'," Heritage Foundation, September 16, 2003; Symposium on "Rethinking 'One China'," Heritage Foundation, February 26, 2004.

[6] "Taiwan Office's Wang Zaixi: Taiwan Independence Means War, Use of Force is Difficult to Avoid," *Xinhua* and *China Daily*, November 18, 2003.

[7] Richard Armitage, press availability, Exhibit Hall, Washington, DC, November 18, 2003.

[8] Interview with the *Washington Post*, published November 23, 2003.

Bush, criticizing his stance as a victory for the authoritarian regime of the PRC at the expense of Taiwan's democratic reforms.[9]

On the TRA's 25th anniversary, the House International Relations Committee held a hearing on April 21, 2004. After congratulating President Chen Shui-bian on his re-election in March 2004, the Administration further clarified U.S. policy toward Taiwan and warned of "limitations" in U.S. support for constitutional changes in Taiwan. At that hearing on the TRA, Representative James Leach, Chairman of the House International Relations Subcommittee on Asia and the Pacific, stated that Taiwan has the unique situation in which it can have de facto self-determination only if it does not attempt to be recognized with de jure sovereignty. He urged Taiwan's people to recognize that they have greater security in "political ambiguity." He called for continuity, saying that "together with our historic 'one China' policy," the TRA has contributed to ensuring peace and stability in the Taiwan Strait.[10] In his second inaugural address on May 20, Chen responded to U.S. concerns, excluding sovereignty issues and a referendum from his plan for a new constitution by 2008. Leach represented the United States at that inauguration. At a subcommittee hearing on June 2, 2004, Leach praised Chen's words as "thoughtful, statesmanlike, and helpful" as well as "constructive" for dialogue with Beijing. To mark the 25th anniversary of the TRA on April 10, 2004, the House voted on July 15, 2004, to pass H.Con.Res. 462 (Hyde) to reaffirm "unwavering commitment" to the TRA.[11]

Congressional also had concerns about **challenges** to U.S. interests in reducing tensions and fostering dialogue across the Taiwan Strait. In March 2005, China adopted an "Anti-Secession Law." On March 16, the House passed (424-4) H.Con.Res. 98 (Hyde) to express grave concern about the "Anti-Secession Law," and the House Taiwan Caucus hosted a briefing by Taiwan's Representative David Lee. On April 6, 2005, the House International Relations Subcommittee on Asia and the Pacific held a hearing on China's "Anti-Secession Law." President Chen announced on February 27, 2006, that he will "terminate" the National Unification Council and Guidelines. Senator John Warner, Chairman of the Armed Services Committee, told Admiral William Fallon, Commander of the Pacific Command, at a committee hearing on March 7, 2006, that "if conflict were precipitated by just inappropriate and wrongful politics generated by the Taiwanese elected officials, I'm not entirely sure that this nation would come full force to their rescue if they created that problem."[12] In July 2007, Representative Tom Lantos, Chairman of the House Foreign Affairs Committee, said that it was impractical for Taiwan to seek membership in the U.N.

With a rhetorical **convergence** among the PRC, Taiwan, and United States on cross-strait "peaceful development" after Ma Ying-jeou became president in Taiwan in May 2008 and cross-strait tension reduced when dialogue resumed, Congressional concerns included issues about whether and how the United States and Taiwan might strengthen bilateral political, security, and economic relations, to sustain U.S. interests in stability, democracy, and prosperity in Taiwan and its international roles. On March 24, 2009, to commemorate the TRA's 30th anniversary, the House passed H.Con.Res. 55, and 30 Senators sent a letter to President Barack Obama. On June 16, 2011, the House Foreign Affairs Committee, chaired by Representative Ileana Ros-Lehtinen, held a hearing on "Why Taiwan Matters." Broad policy issues include whether to review U.S.

---

[9] Sherrod Brown, Steve Chabot, Dana Rohrabacher, and Robert Wexler, "Congressional Taiwan Caucus Urges President Bush to Reconsider Position on Taiwanese Referendum," December 11, 2003.

[10] House International Relations Committee, hearing, "The Taiwan Relations Act: the Next 25 Years," April 21, 2004.

[11] The vote was 400 yeas, 18 nays, 4 present, and 11 not-voting.

[12] Senate Armed Services Committee, Hearing on the FY2007 Defense Department Budget, March 7, 2006.

policy in view of significant changes since the last policy review that took place in 1994. Some have said that the improved cross-strait engagement helps U.S. attention to shift to expanding cooperation from a rising China. Congress also could conduct oversight of the State Department's restrictions on contacts between Executive Branch officials and Taiwan's officials in the "Guidelines on Relations with Taiwan" to carry out only an "unofficial" relationship.[13] Others have argued that the self-imposed restrictions go beyond the TRA (which did not stipulate an "unofficial" relationship), the reality of official contacts, or the U.S.-PRC communiques. They also have concerns that the restrictions undermine communication with and denigrate Taiwan. Another issue has been whether to resume Cabinet-level visits to Taiwan that took place from 1992 to 2000.

Table 1. Cabinet-Level Visits to Taiwan After 1979

1992	U.S. Trade Representative Carla Hills
1994	Secretary of Transportation Federico Pena
1996	Small Business Administrator Phil Lader
1998	Secretary of Energy Bill Richardson
2000	Secretary of Transportation Rodney Slater

Source: U.S.-Taiwan Business Council, sponsor of economic conferences.

In sum, Congress has exercised important roles in legislating and overseeing the TRA of 1979, as Congress and the President have recalibrated the U.S. "one China" policy over the decades. Since the mid-1990s, U.S. interests in the military balance as well as peace and stability in the Taiwan Strait have been challenged by the PRC's military modernization, resistance in Taiwan by the Kuomintang (KMT) party to raising defense spending (including to buy U.S. arms), and moves perceived by Beijing as promoting *de jure* independence under the Democratic Progressive Party (DPP) (when Chen Shui-bian was President in 2000-2008). Moreover, since 2000, political polarization in Taiwan has raised the importance of U.S. policy toward Taiwan for fostering U.S. interests there. These interests include sustainable peace and security for the people of Taiwan (with a global impact), Taiwan's democracy, and economic ties with a major trading partner—ultimately a "peaceful resolution" of the dispute over Taiwan. At the same time, the dominance of domestic politics in Taiwan has reduced U.S. leverage to advance some U.S. priorities. U.S. policy respects democracies, but U.S. actions and words could impact those internal politics.

Key Statements and Ambiguity

Five key documents stand out among U.S. policy statements on Taiwan:

- Shanghai Communique of 1972

- Normalization Communique of 1979

- Taiwan Relations Act (TRA) (P.L. 96-8) of 1979

- Six Assurances to Taipei of 1982

- August 17 Communique (on arms sales) of 1982.

---

[13] State Department, memorandum, "Guidelines on Relations with Taiwan," March 4, 2011.

(See excerpts of these and other statements in Part II of this CRS report.)

Despite apparently consistent formal statements and closed-door assurances since the end of World War II (and the end of Taiwan's status as a colony of Japan that began in 1895), the "one China" question has been left somewhat ambiguous and subject to different interpretations among Washington, Beijing, and Taipei. The concept of "one China" has been complicated by the co-existence of the PRC government ruling the mainland and the ROC government on Taiwan since 1949. Taiwan was never ruled by the Communist Party of China (CPC) or as part of the PRC.

Changed Context

The political and strategic context of those key statements also has experienced significant change. After political liberalization began in 1986, Taiwan became a democracy, with a new basis for the government's legitimacy and greater say by proponents of a separate status for Taiwan. The PRC's Tiananmen Crackdown of 1989 dramatically proved the limits to liberal change on the mainland. The original strategic rationale for U.S.-PRC rapprochement faded with the end of the Cold War. In May 2000, the Democratic Progressive Party (DPP)'s Chen Shui-bian became President of the ROC, ousting the Nationalist Party of China, or Kuomintang (KMT), as the ruling party in Taiwan for the first time in 55 years.

Definitions

There are complications about the language in the key statements. First, "China" was not defined in the three joint communiques. In the Normalization Communique, the United States recognized the PRC government as the sole legal government of China, but the PRC has never ruled Taiwan and other islands under the control of the ROC government. The PRC's late paramount leader Deng Xiaoping's 1984 proposal of "one China, two systems" sought to define Taiwan as a Special Administrative Region under the PRC after unification. On the other hand, "Taiwan" was defined in Section 15(2) of the TRA essentially to be the islands of Taiwan and the Pescadores, plus the people, entities, and governing authorities there.

Unsettled Status

Second, there has been disagreement as to whether Taiwan's status actually was resolved or determined. In secret talks in 1972, President Nixon assured PRC Premier Zhou Enlai that the United States viewed the status of Taiwan as "determined" to be part of one China. The PRC's December 1978 statement on normalization of diplomatic relations with the United States said that the Taiwan question "has now been resolved between the two countries." However, the U.S. statement of December 1978 on normalization stated the expectation that the Taiwan question "will be settled" peacefully by the Chinese themselves. The TRA also stipulated the U.S. expectation that the future of Taiwan "will be determined" by peaceful means. President Reagan's 1982 statement on arms sales to Taiwan declared that "the Taiwan question is a matter for the Chinese people, on both sides of the Taiwan Strait, to resolve." Moreover, under U.S. policy, "settlement" or "resolution"—not stated as "unification" or "reunification"—of the Taiwan question is left open to be peacefully determined by both sides of the strait. In a rare public statement on this U.S. stance, in August 2007, a National Security Council official said that "the position of the United States Government is that the ROC—Republic of China—is an issue undecided ... for many, many years."[14]

Peaceful Settlement

Third, the questions of the PRC's possible use of force, U.S. arms sales to Taiwan, and possible U.S. help in Taiwan's self-defense were left contentious and critical for U.S. interests. Washington consistently has stated its strong interest that there be a peaceful settlement, but the PRC has not renounced its claimed sovereign right to use force if necessary. Washington has not promised to end arms sales to Taiwan, although the Mutual Defense Treaty of 1954 was terminated on December 31, 1979.[15] In the surprise announcements of December 1978 on diplomatic recognition, the United States stated its interest in a peaceful resolution, but the PRC countered that Taiwan is China's internal affair. President Reagan agreed to the 1982 Communique on reducing U.S. arms sales to Taiwan—premised on the PRC's declared policy of peaceful unification. In the early 1990s, the PLA began to build up its theater missile force and to acquire modern arms, especially from Moscow.

The 1979 TRA states that the United States will provide necessary defense articles and services to Taiwan for its sufficient self-defense, and will consider with "grave concern" any non-peaceful means to determine Taiwan's future. In deciding on that language in 1979, Members of Congress debated whether the wording on U.S. military intentions was clear or ambiguous. Since the mid-1990s, a new debate has arisen over how to deter conflict in the Taiwan Strait, including whether ambiguity or clarity in U.S. statements about a possible military role serves U.S. interests in preventing conflict or provocations from either Beijing or Taipei.[16] There have been issues about whether and how U.S. statements of intentions might be clarified to specify the conditions under which the U.S. military might help to defend Taiwan and the U.S. stance on Taiwan's sovereignty or efforts to change its declared political status.[17] Questions also have persisted about the extent of the U.S. defense commitment to Taiwan, given President Clinton's 1996 deployment of two aircraft carriers near Taiwan and President Bush's initial statement in 2001 of doing "whatever it took to help Taiwan defend herself."

Has U.S. Policy Changed?

Apart from questions about the language in the key statements on "one China," policy questions have arisen about whether successive Administrations have changed the U.S. position since 1971 to adapt to changing circumstances and whether such shifts have advanced U.S. interests.[18]

---

[14] Dennis Wilder, Senior Director for Asian Affairs, NSC, White House, "Press Briefing on the President's Trip to Australia and the APEC Summit," August 30, 2007.

[15] Article 10 of the Mutual Defense Treaty allowed for its termination one year after notice is given by either side (on January 1, 1979).

[16] In the 106th Congress, the House International Relations Committee debated this issue of "ambiguity" and other issues in the markup of H.R. 1838, "Taiwan Security Enhancement Act," October 26, 1999.

[17] See for example: Joseph Nye, Jr., "A Taiwan Deal," *Washington Post*, March 8, 1998; Heritage Foundation and Project for the New American Century, "Statement on the Defense of Taiwan" by 23 conservatives, including Richard Armitage and Paul Wolfowitz, August 20, 1999; Thomas Christensen, "Clarity on Taiwan," *Washington Post*, March 20, 2000; Richard Bush, "American Ambiguity on Taiwan's Sovereignty Increases the Island's Safety," *Insight Magazine*, December 10, 2002.

[18] While this report discusses U.S. policy since the first understanding with the PRC in 1971, some say that the U.S. (continued...)

Successive Administrations have generally maintained that "long-standing" U.S. policy has been consistent. Some in Congress and others, however, have contended that U.S. policy has changed in some important areas. There also are issues as to whether any elements of the "one China" policy should be reviewed for modification. The "one China" policy has evolved to cover three issue areas: sovereignty, use of force, and cross-strait dialogue.

Issue Area 1: Sovereignty

One issue area for U.S. policy concerns sovereignty, including Taiwan's juridical status, future unification vs. independence, referendums, a new constitution, and international participation. The U.S. "one China" *policy* has differed from the PRC's *principle* on "one China," and there have been questions about whether U.S. policy is one of support, non-support, or opposition to unification or independence. In short, U.S. policy has stressed the *process* (peaceful resolution, cross-strait dialogue, with the assent of Taiwan's people, and no provocations or unilateral changes by either side) rather than the *outcome* (e.g., unification, independence, confederation). At the same time, the ROC, or Taiwan, has continued to assert its sovereignty, seek membership in the United Nations and other international organizations. Moreover, under the ruling DPP since 2000, the government in Taipei has made greater use of the name "Taiwan" (vs. "ROC").[19]

Even while recognizing the ROC government and its "jurisdiction" over Taiwan, on the eve of the Nixon Administration's contacts with PRC leaders in Beijing, the State Department testified to Congress in 1969 and 1970 that the juridical matter of the status of Taiwan remained undetermined. The State Department also wrote that

> In neither [the Japanese Peace Treaty of 1951 nor the Treaty of Peace between the Republic of China and Japan of 1952] did Japan cede this area [of Formosa and the Pescadores] to any particular entity. As Taiwan and the Pescadores are not covered by any existing international

---

(...continued)

position on "one China" dates back to World War II. (See Henry Kissinger, "Storm Clouds Gathering," *Washington Post*, September 7, 1999.) In Taiwan after World War II, October 25, 1945, or "Retrocession Day," marked the Republic of China (ROC)'s claim of "recovering" Taiwan (then called Formosa) from Japan. However, that was the first time that the ROC's forces had been on Formosa to occupy it, upon Japan's surrender. When the Qing Empire ceded in perpetuity Formosa to Japan under the Treaty of Shimonoseki of 1895, the ROC was not in existence. Moreover, Formosa's people did not have a say in determining their status. The Kuomintang (KMT), or Nationalist Party of China, has contended that the ROC claimed Formosa at Japan's surrender in August 1945, with no country challenging the island's status (see Stephen Chen, former ROC representative to Washington in 1997-2000, "Taiwan Belongs to the Republic of China," paper given to author in March 2008). Following the ROC government's retreat to Taiwan in 1949 and the start of the Korean War, the U.S. stance shifted on sovereignty over Taiwan. On January 5, 1950, President Truman stated that the United States would not get involved in the civil conflict in China. After the Korean War started, however, President Truman declared on June 27, 1950, that "the occupation of Formosa by Communist forces would be a direct threat to the security of the Pacific area and to United States forces performing their lawful and necessary functions in that area." The President said that he ordered the 7th Fleet to prevent any attack on Formosa and also called upon the ROC government on Formosa to cease all air and sea operations against the mainland. President Truman added that "the determination of the future status of Formosa must await the restoration of security in the Pacific, a peace settlement with Japan, or consideration by the United Nations." (Quoted in: Senate Foreign Relations Subcommittee on U.S. Security Agreements and Commitments Abroad, record of hearing on November 24, 1969; and Alan Romberg, *Rein in at the Brink of the Precipice*, Stimson Center, 2003).

[19] Such as: the addition of "Taiwan" in the title of the ROC Yearbook; the addition of "Taiwan" in English on ROC passports beginning on September 1, 2003; changing the title of a government publication, *Taipei Review*, to *Taiwan Review* beginning with the March 2003 issue; and requests to use "Taiwan" instead of "Taipei" in the names of representative offices in the United States and other countries. In April 2007, Taiwan unsuccessfully applied for membership in the World Health Organization under the name "Taiwan."

---

disposition, sovereignty over the area is an unsettled question subject to future international resolution. Both the Republic of China and the Chinese Communists disagree with this conclusion and consider that Taiwan and the Pescadores are part of the sovereign state of China. The United States recognizes the Government of the Republic of China as legitimately occupying and exercising jurisdiction over Taiwan and the Pescadores.[20]

However, accounts of President Nixon's secret talks with PRC Premier Zhou Enlai in China in 1972 reported that Nixon made promises on the question of Taiwan in return for diplomatic normalization that went beyond the communique issued at the end. The Carter Administration later called the promises: "Nixon's Five Points."[21] Also, according to Assistant Secretary of State Stanley Roth's March 1999 testimony, Nixon pledged no U.S. support for Taiwan independence (second time after Kissinger's 1971 promise): "We have not and will not support any Taiwan independence movement."[22] With the release on December 11, 2003, of declassified memoranda of conversation of the secret talks between Nixon and Zhou, there was confirmation that Nixon stated as first of Five Principles that "there is one China, and Taiwan is a part of China. There will be no more statements made—if I can control our bureaucracy—to the effect that the status of Taiwan is undetermined."

The United States did not explicitly state its own position on the status of Taiwan in the three U.S.-PRC Joint Communiques. In 1972, while still recognizing the ROC, the Nixon Administration declared that it "acknowledges" that "all Chinese on both sides of the Taiwan Strait" maintain that there is one China and Taiwan is a part of China, and that the United States did not challenge that position. After shifting diplomatic recognition to the PRC, the United States, in 1979 and 1982, again "acknowledged the Chinese position"[23] of one China and Taiwan is part of China. However, the 1982 communique further stated that the United States has no intention of pursuing a policy of "two Chinas" or "one China, one Taiwan," while President Reagan's accompanying statement said that "the Taiwan question is a matter for the Chinese people, on both sides of the Taiwan Strait, to resolve." The TRA did not discuss the "one China" concept. In 1994, the Clinton Administration stated after its Taiwan Policy Review that the United States had "acknowledged" the Chinese position on one China and that "since 1978, each Administration has reaffirmed this policy."

Despite these apparent similarities in U.S. policy statements, some contend that the U.S. position, since originally formulated in 1972, has adopted the PRC's "one China" principle—rather than steadily maintaining neutrality and equal distance from Beijing and Taipei. In 1982, Senator John Glenn criticized both the Carter and Reagan Administrations:

---

[20] Senate Foreign Relations Subcommittee on U.S. Security Agreements and Commitments Abroad, hearings on the Republic of China, November 24, 25, 26, 1969, and May 8, 1970. Also: State Department memorandum on the legal status of Taiwan, July 13, 1971, a copy of which Nat Bellochi, former chairman of AIT, provided.

[21] James Mann, *About Face: A History of America's Curious Relationship with China, From Nixon to Clinton* (New York: Alfred A. Knopf, 1999), p. 46; Harding, Harry, *A Fragile Relationship: The United States and China Since 1972* (Washington: Brookings Institution, 1992), p. 43-44. According to Holdridge, Nixon reiterated the position against an independent Taiwan that Kissinger told Zhou in July 1971.

[22] Senate Foreign Relations Committee, hearing on United States-Taiwan Relations: The 20th Anniversary of the Taiwan Relations Act, March 25, 1999, written response to Senator Helms' question about precedents for President Clinton's June 1998 "Three Noes" statement, citing a Memorandum of Conversation, Tuesday, February 22, 1972, 2:10 pm-6:00 pm (declassified version).

[23] The Chinese text said "recognized China's position."

The ambiguous formulation agreed upon in the 1979 joint communique went considerably further in recognizing the PRC's claim to Taiwan. Although the word "acknowledged" remained, the object of our acknowledgment shifted noticeably. We no longer just acknowledged that both Chinas asserted the principle that there was one China, but instead acknowledged the Chinese position that there is but one China. By dropping the key phrase "all Chinese on either side of the Taiwan Strait maintain" one could interpret that we had moved from the position of neutral bystander noting the existence of a dispute, to a party accepting the Chinese assertion that there is one China. Clearly, this was the PRC's interpretation.... More recently, Peking's threats to downgrade relations with the United States, unless Washington agreed to end all arms sales to Taiwan, prompted President Reagan to write to China's Communist Party Chairman, Hu Yaobang, in May 1982, and assure him that, "Our policy will continue to be based on the principle that there is but one China...." We now assert that it is our policy, U.S. policy, that there is but one China, and although not stated, indicate implicitly that Taiwan is a part of that one China. The use of the qualifier "acknowledged" has been dropped altogether.... I do not believe that anyone can dispute that the U.S. policy toward China and Taiwan has changed dramatically over the last 10 years. Let me reiterate one more time, in 1972, we acknowledged that the Chinese on both sides of the Taiwan Strait maintained that there was but one China. Today it is U.S. policy that there is but one China. Despite this remarkable shift over time, the State Department, at each juncture, has assured us that our policy remained essentially unchanged.[24]

Clinton's Three Noes

In August 1995—earlier than the first public statements showed in 1997—President Clinton reportedly sent a secret letter to PRC President Jiang Zemin in which he stated as the U.S. position that we would: (1) "oppose" Taiwan independence; (2) would not support "two Chinas" or one China and one Taiwan; and (3) would not support Taiwan's admission to the United Nations.[25] The opposition to Taiwan independence seemed to go beyond the promises made by former National Security Advisor Henry Kissinger and President Nixon in 1971 and 1972 of no U.S. support for Taiwan independence. Later, that wording was apparently changed from opposition to a neutral stance of non-support. This letter reportedly formed the basis of what were later known publicly as the "Three Noes."

At the 1997 Clinton-Jiang summit in Washington, the two leaders issued a joint statement which included a U.S. position: "the United States reiterates that it adheres to its 'one China' policy and the principles set forth in the three U.S.-China joint communiques." While that joint statement did not include the "Three Noes," the Administration decided to have a State Department spokesperson say two days later that "we certainly made clear that we have a one-China policy; that we don't support a one-China, one-Taiwan policy. We don't support a two-China policy. We don't support Taiwan independence, and we don't support Taiwanese membership in organizations that require you to be a member state." While in China for a summit in June 1998, President Clinton chose an informal forum to declare: "I had a chance to reiterate our Taiwan policy, which is that we don't support independence for Taiwan, or two Chinas, or one Taiwan-

---

[24] Statement of Hon. John Glenn, U.S. Senator from Ohio, on China-Taiwan Policy, July 22, 1982, in: Lester L. Wolff and David L. Simon, *Legislative History of the Taiwan Relations Act* (New York: American Association for Chinese Studies, 1982), p. 306-307.

[25] Garver, John W., *Face Off: China, the United States, and Taiwan's Democratization* (University of Washington Press, 1997); James Mann, *About Face: A History of America's Curious Relationship with China, From Nixon to Clinton* (New York: Alfred A. Knopf, 1999).

one China. And we don't believe that Taiwan should be a member in any organization for which statehood is a requirement."

Some questioned whether the "Three Noes," especially as it was publicly declared by the U.S. President while in the PRC, was a change in U.S. policy.[26] U.S. non-support for a one China, one Taiwan; or two Chinas can be traced to the private assurances of the Nixon Administration in the early 1970s. However, the Clinton Administration, beginning with its Taiwan Policy Review of 1994, added non-support for Taipei's entry into the United Nations (U.N.), which became an issue after Taipei launched its bid in 1993. In response to President Clinton's "Three Noes," concerned Members in both the Senate and the House nearly unanimously passed resolutions in July 1998, reaffirming the U.S. commitment to Taiwan.

The Clinton Administration, nonetheless, argued that the "Three Noes" did not represent a change in policy. Testifying before the Senate Foreign Relations Committee on March 25, 1999, Assistant Secretary of State Stanley Roth stated that "every point made there [in the "Three Noes"] had been made before by a previous Administration and there was no change whatsoever." In a written response to a question from Senator Helms, Roth cited as precedents for the "Three Noes" a 1971 statement by Kissinger, a 1972 statement by Nixon, a 1979 statement by Deputy Secretary of State Warren Christopher, and President Reagan's 1982 Communique.

Bush on Taiwan's Independence, Referendums, Constitution

On April 25, 2001, when President George W. Bush stated the U.S. commitment to Taiwan as an obligation to use "whatever it took to help Taiwan defend herself," he also said that "a declaration of independence is not the one China policy, and we will work with Taiwan to make sure that that doesn't happen." Visiting Beijing in February 2002, Bush said that U.S. policy on Taiwan was unchanged, but he emphasized U.S. commitment to the TRA and a peaceful resolution, along with opposition to provocations by either Beijing or Taipei. After Taiwan President Chen Shui-bian said on August 3, 2002, that there is "one country on each side" of the Taiwan Strait, the U.S. National Security Council (NSC) stated, in a second response, that "we do not support Taiwan independence." With Jiang Zemin at his side at a summit in Crawford, TX, in October 2002, President Bush himself stated that "we do not support independence."

However, there have been questions about whether the Bush Administration adjusted U.S. policy after President Chen Shui-bian surprised the United States in August 2002 with a speech on "one country on each side" and a call for a holding referendums. Specifically, there was the issue of whether President Bush gave assurances, at closed meetings starting at that summit in October 2002, to PRC President Jiang Zemin and later President Hu Jintao that the United States was "against" or "opposed" (vs. non-support of) unilateral moves in Taiwan toward independence and/or the status of Taiwan independence, in the interest of stability in the Taiwan Strait.[27] A position in "opposition" to Taiwan independence would represent a shift in policy focus from the

---

[26] For example: Stephen J. Yates, "Clinton Statement Undermines Taiwan," Heritage Foundation, July 10, 1998; Ted Galen Carpenter, "Let Taiwan Defend Itself," Policy Analysis, Cato Institute, August 24, 1998; Stephen J. Yates, "Promoting Freedom and Security in U.S.-Taiwan Policy," Heritage Foundation, October 13, 1998; James Lilley and Arthur Waldron, "Taiwan is a 'State,' Get Over It," *Wall Street Journal*, July 14, 1999; Harvey J. Feldman, "How Washington Can Defuse Escalating Tensions in the Taiwan Strait," Heritage Foundation, August 19, 1999.

[27] According to the *Far Eastern Economic Review* (April 22, 2004), President Bush met with his AIT officials, Therese Shaheen and Douglas Paal, in the summer of 2003 on policy toward Taiwan, and Bush said "I'm not a nuance guy— 'Do not support.' 'Oppose.' It's the same to me."

process to the outcome and go beyond President Nixon's "Five Principles," which expressed the neutral stance of "non-support" for Taiwan independence. But U.S. opposition to Taiwan independence would be consistent with President Clinton's secret letter reportedly sent in 1995 to PRC leader Jiang Zemin, as the basis for the "Three Noes." U.S. opposition would also conflict with the stance of the government of Taiwan, which, under the DPP, argued that Taiwan is already independent, as evident since the first democratic presidential election in 1996.[28]

After Chen, during campaigns for Taiwan's presidential election in March 2004, advocated holding referendums and adopting a new constitution by 2008—moves that could have implications for Taiwan's sovereignty and cross-strait stability, the Bush Administration called on Chen to adhere to his pledges ("Five Noes") in his inaugural address of 2000 (including not promoting a referendum to change the status quo). On September 28, 2003, Chen started his call for a new constitution for Taiwan (with a draft constitution by September 28, 2006; a referendum on the constitution on December 10, 2006; and enactment of the new constitution on May 20, 2008). National Security Advisor Condoleezza Rice said on October 14, 2003, that "nobody should try unilaterally to change the status quo."[29] A White House official said in an interview on November 26, 2003, that "Taiwan shouldn't be moving towards independence; and mainland China shouldn't be moving towards the use of force or coercion."[30] Then, Chen announced on November 29—two days after the opposition-dominated legislature passed a restrictive law authorizing referendums—that he would still use one provision to hold a "defensive referendum" on election day.[31] Chen argued that the referendum would be a way for Taiwan's people to express their opposition to the PLA's missile threat and would have nothing to do with the question of unification or independence.

Nonetheless, Administration officials had concerns about the volatile course of current and future political actions in Taiwan (with elections, referendums, and a new constitution), reforms geared for governance vs sovereignty, and unnecessary effects on peace and stability, given U.S. commitments to help Taiwan's self-defense. The Bush Administration added a new, clearer stance on December 1, 2003, when the State Department expressed U.S. "opposition" to any referendum that would change Taiwan's status or move toward independence. On the same day, the Senior Director of Asian Affairs at the White House's National Security Council, James Moriarty, reportedly was in Taiwan to pass a letter from Bush to Chen with concerns about "provocations."[32] Apparently needing a public, stronger, and clearer U.S. message to Taiwan, appearing next to visiting PRC Premier Wen Jiabao at the White House on December 9, 2003, President Bush stated opposition to any unilateral decision by China or Taiwan to change the

---

[28] Chen Ming-tong, a Vice Chairman of the Mainland Affairs Council in Taiwan, spoke at a conference of the Global Alliance for Democracy and Peace in Houston, TX, on October 31, 2003, and contended that Taiwan is already a sovereign, democratic country that is in a "post-independence period" and does not need to declare independence. Joseph Wu, Deputy Secretary General of the Presidential Office of Chen Shui-bian, wrote in *Taipei Times* on January 6, 2004, that Taiwan's independence is the "new status quo."

[29] Previously, Secretary of State Warren Christopher stated in May 1996—two months after President Clinton deployed two aircraft carriers near Taiwan and days before an inauguration address by Taiwan's President Lee Teng-hui—that "we have emphasized to both sides the importance of avoiding provocative actions or unilateral measures that would alter the status quo or pose a threat to peaceful resolution of outstanding issues."

[30] Background interview with Senior White House Official, *Phoenix TV*, November 26, 2003.

[31] Article 17 of the referendum law passed on November 27, 2003, in the Legislative Yuan authorizes the president to initiate a referendum on national security issues "if the country suffers an external threat that causes concern that national sovereignty will change."

[32] *Lien-Ho Pao [United Daily News]*, Taipei, December 1, 2003; *New York Times*, December 9, 2003.

status quo, as well as opposition to efforts by Taiwan's President Chen to change the status quo, in response to a question about whether Chen should cancel the referendum.

However, Bush did not make public remarks against the PRC's threats toward democratic Taiwan. Bush also did not counter Wen's remarks that Bush reiterated "opposition" to Taiwan independence. Bush raised questions about whether he miscalculated the willingness of Chen to back down during his re-election campaign and risked U.S. credibility, since Chen responded defiantly that he would hold the "anti-missile, anti-war" referendums as planned and that his intention was to keep Taiwan's current independent status quo from being changed.[33]

American opinions were divided on the Bush Administration's statements toward Taiwan. Some saw Chen as advancing a provocative agenda of permanent separation from China while trying to win votes, and supported Bush's forceful stance against Chen's plan for referendums.[34] Others criticized President Bush for being one-sided in appeasing a dictatorship at the expense of Taiwan's democracy while failing to warn against and even possibly inviting aggression from Beijing.[35] The co-chairmen of the Congressional Taiwan Caucus in the House wrote a letter to President Bush, criticizing his stance as a victory for the authoritarian regime of the PRC at the expense of Taiwan's democratic reforms.[36] Some critics argued for a new approach, saying that the "one China" policy became "irrelevant" and that there were national security interests in preventing the "unification" of Taiwan with China.[37] In contrast, another opinion advocated the continuation of arms sales to Taiwan with no position on its independence and staying out of any conflict in the Taiwan Strait.[38]

Still, uncertainty remained about the Bush Administration's implementation of U.S. policy on questions such as options to recalibrate policy in exercising leverage over Taipei or Beijing; capacity to maintain the delicate balance in preventing provocations by either side of the strait rather than swerving to one side or another; perceptions in Taipei and Beijing of mixed messages from Washington; the U.S. stance on referendums and a new constitution in Taiwan; definition of "status quo"; deference to democracy in Taiwan; Taiwan's long-standing, de facto independence from China; stronger separate national identity in Taiwan; a proactive U.S. political role (such as urging dialogue, facilitating talks, or mediating negotiations) in addition to proactive pressures on

---

[33] Chen Shui-bian responded to Bush in a meeting with visiting Representative Dan Burton on December 10, 2003, reported *Taipei Times*, December 11, 2003; and Chen's meeting with author and others at the Presidential Palace, Taipei, December 11, 2003.

[34] See *Wall Street Journal*, "The End of Ambiguity," editorial, December 10, 2003; Ross Munro, "Blame Taiwan," *National Review*, December 18, 2003; Peter Brookes (Heritage Foundation), "Why Bush Acted on Taiwan," *Far Eastern Economic Review*, December 25, 2003; Michael Swaine, "Trouble in Taiwan," *Foreign Affairs*, March/April 2004.

[35] For example, William Kristol, Robert Kagan, Gary Schmitt (Project for the New American Century), "U.S.-China-Taiwan Policy," December 9, 2003; *Washington Post*, "Mr. Bush's Kowtow," editorial, December 10, 2003; and Robert Kagan and William Kristol, "Stand by Taiwan," *Weekly Standard*, December 22, 2003.

[36] Sherrod Brown, Steve Chabot, Dana Rohrabacher, and Robert Wexler, "Congressional Taiwan Caucus Urges President Bush to Reconsider Position on Taiwanese Referendum," December 11, 2003.

[37] For example, conference at the Heritage Foundation, "Rethinking 'One China'," February 26, 2004; and Thomas Donnelly, "Taiwan: Test Case of the Bush Doctrine," AEI, National Security Outlook, April 2004.

[38] Ted Galen Carpenter, "President Bush's Muddled Policy on Taiwan," CATO Institute, Foreign Policy Briefing, March 15, 2004.

defense; the extent of the U.S. commitment to assist Taiwan's self-defense; the increasing PLA threat; and U.S. worries about Taiwan's defense spending, acquisitions, and the will to fight.[39]

On January 16, 2004, President Chen provided the wording for the two questions, saying that the referendums will ask citizens (1) whether the government should acquire more missile defense systems if the Chinese Communists do not withdraw missiles and renounce the use of force against Taiwan, and (2) whether the government should negotiate with the Chinese Communists to establish a framework for cross-strait peace and stability. Chen also promised that if re-elected, he will maintain "the status quo of cross-strait peace."[40] On election day on March 20, 2004, the two referendums failed to be considered valid when 45% of eligible voters cast ballots (less than the 50% needed).

After the election in March 2004, the White House sent the Senior Director for Asian Affairs, Michael Green, to Taiwan to urge President Chen to exclude sovereignty-related issues from constitutional changes.[41] In testimony by Assistant Secretary of State James Kelly on April 21, 2004, the Bush Administration warned Chen of "limitations" in U.S. support for constitutional changes in Taiwan. In his inaugural address on May 20, 2004, Chen responded to a number of U.S. concerns.

In President Chen's second term, President Bush did not support Taiwan's independence or membership in the U.N. and opposed unilateral changes to the "status quo." Leading up to Taiwan's presidential election on March 22, 2008, Bush Administration officials expressed opposition to referendums on Taiwan's membership in the U.N. that were held on the same day.

Visits (or Transits) by Taiwan's President

One policy question has concerned the appropriate U.S. response to requests from Taiwan's president to enter the United States for official visits, private visits, or extended transits; to visit Washington, DC; and to meet with officials and Members of Congress. Congress has expressed strong support for granting such visits. Since 1994, the U.S. response has evolved from initially denying Lee Teng-hui entry into the United States to relaxing restrictions on "transits" for visits by Chen Shui-bian, and back to strict conditions for Chen's transits in May 2006.

In May 1994, the Clinton Administration allowed President Lee Teng-hui to make a refueling stop in Hawaii but denied him a visa. In 1995, Lee received a visa to visit Cornell University, his alma mater. (Beijing responded with PLA exercises and missile launches in 1995 and 1996.) Congress' view was an important factor acknowledged by the Administration in its reversal of policy to grant the visa.

In August 2000, the Clinton Administration granted a visa to the newly-elected President Chen Shui-bian to transit in Los Angeles on his way to South America and Africa, but, according to

---

[39] Based in part on the author's visit to Taiwan, December 5-13, 2003. Also, for critiques in a longer-term context, see for example: Bates Gill (Center for Strategic and International Studies), "Bush Was Correct but Clumsy on Taiwan Policy," *Financial Times*, December 12, 2003; Kenneth Lieberthal (University of Michigan), "Dire Strait: The Risks on Taiwan," *Washington Post*, January 8, 2004.

[40] President of the Republic of China, news releases (in Chinese and English), January 16, 2004. Chen's use of the phrase "the status quo of cross-strait peace" was translated simply as "status quo" in the official English version.

[41] Susan Lawrence, "Bush to Taiwan: Don't Risk It," *Far Eastern Economic Review*, May 20, 2004.

Taiwan's Foreign Ministry, Washington and Taipei had an understanding that Chen would not hold public events. Representative Sam Gejdenson organized a meeting between Chen and about 15 Members of Congress (some of whom were in town for the Democratic National Convention), but Chen told them he was "unavailable."[42]

In 2001, in granting President Chen Shui-bian "private and unofficial" transits through New York (May 21-23) and Houston (June 2-3) en route to and from Latin America, the Bush Administration took a different position on such meetings. As the State Department spokesperson said, "we do believe that private meetings between Members of Congress and foreign leaders advance our national interests, so [Chen] may have meetings with Members of Congress."[43] On the night of May 21, 2001, 21 Representatives attended a dinner with Chen in New York, and Representative Tom DeLay later hosted Chen in Houston.

In 2003, while considering his safety, comfort, convenience, and dignity, the Bush Administration again granted President Chen's requests for transits to and from Panama through New York (October 31-November 2) and Anchorage (November 4-5).[44] Some Members of Congress personally welcomed Chen, including 16 Members who were already in New York and met with him. No Administration officials met with Chen, other than AIT officials based in Washington. Deputy Assistant Secretary of State Randall Schriver reportedly canceled a planned meeting with Chen in New York, and Deputy Secretary of State Richard Armitage talked with Chen by phone.[45]

Chen Shui-bian enjoyed extended transits through Honolulu and Seattle in August-September 2004, though these were less high-profile than that in New York. In January 2005, Chen stopped in Guam on the way back to Taiwan from Palau and the Solomon Islands. In September 2005, the Bush Administration allowed Chen to stop one day in Miami on his way to Latin America and in San Francisco on his return to Taiwan. The Congressional Human Rights Caucus, via teleconference, awarded Chen a human rights award while he was in Miami.

However, in May 2006, the Bush Administration was not pleased at repeated statements from President Chen Shui-bian and responded by tightening restrictions on his proposed U.S. stops so that they would be strict transits (with no activities), conditions similar to those for Lee Teng-hui in 1994. Chen requested stops in San Francisco and New York for his visit to Latin America, but President Bush countered with transits in Honolulu and Anchorage, and Chen refused those U.S. cities. Representatives Thomas Tancredo and Dana Rohrabacher sent a letter on May 5, 2006, to Secretary of State Condoleezza Rice, questioning the decision's consistency with legislation; possible linkage to ties with Beijing; use of "humiliating" conditions on the transits; reversal of policy despite President Bush's affirmation of a consistent policy; impact on future U.S. stops; and implication for "playing politics" given the contrast with Deputy Secretary of State Robert Zoellick's high-level meeting in Washington with the opposition KMT chairman, Ma Ying-jeou, two months earlier. In September 2006, the Administration allowed Chen to stop in Guam, but he had to switch to a civilian aircraft instead of his "Air Force One" that flew him to Palau.

---

[42] *Central News Agency* (Taipei), August 9, 2000; "Taiwan Leader Stops in Los Angeles," *Washington Post*, August 14, 2000; Sam Gejdenson, "Taiwan Deserves Better: Why We Should Have Met with President Chen," *Washington Times*, August 21, 2000.

[43] Department of State, press briefing by Richard Boucher, May 14, 2001.

[44] Department of State, press briefing by Richard Boucher, October 7, 2003.

[45] Susan Lawrence, "Diplomatic But Triumphal Progress," *Far Eastern Economic Review*, November 13, 2003.

In January 2007, the Administration allowed President Chen to stop overnight in San Francisco and to refuel in Los Angeles on his way to and from Nicaragua. In response to restrictions on Chen's transits, Representative Dana Rohrabacher and 14 other Members wrote a letter to House Speaker Nancy Pelosi on January 12, 2007, calling for the removal of all restrictions on bilateral high-level visits with Taiwan. A week later, Representative Tancredo criticized (in extension of remarks) Mexico's ban of Chen's plane from Mexican airspace on his way to Los Angeles, a move similar to U.S. treatment toward Taiwan. In August 2007, the Administration restricted Chen's transits to 50-minute refueling stops in Anchorage on his way to and from Central America, with no overnight stays. For his last U.S. transit in January 2008, the Bush Administration allowed Chen to stop in Anchorage for two hours to refuel and rest.

After Ma Ying-jeou won the election on March 22, 2008, he expressed a desire to visit the United States before his inauguration in May (after which U.S. policy would allow only transits). But the Bush Administration denied his request. President Ma has sought limited goals in U.S. transits.

World Health Organization (WHO)

The United States, with strong congressional backing, has voiced some support for Taiwan's quest for international space, including "meaningful participation" in certain international organizations on transnational issues. Some advocates view such participation as preserving a democratic government's international presence and promoting the interests of Taiwan's people, while others support Taiwan's separate identity or independence. The Clinton Administration's 1994 Taiwan Policy Review promised to support Taiwan's membership in organizations where statehood is not a prerequisite and to support opportunities for Taiwan's voice to be heard in organizations where its membership is not possible.

The focus of Taiwan's international participation was at the World Health Organization (WHO), and the annual meetings in May in Geneva of its governing body, the World Health Assembly (WHA). On May 11, 2001, President Bush wrote to Senator Frank Murkowski, agreeing that the Administration should "find opportunities for Taiwan's voice to be heard in organizations in order to make a contribution, even if membership is impossible," including concrete ways for Taiwan to benefit from and contribute to the WHO. On April 9, 2002, Representatives in the House formed a Taiwan Caucus, and, as its first action, it wrote a letter on April 19, 2002, to the President, seeking support for Taiwan's participation in the WHO. With worldwide attention on the severe acute respiratory syndrome (SARS) epidemic, Secretary of Health and Human Services Tommy Thompson expressed support for Taiwan in a speech at the WHA on May 19, 2003, saying that "the need for effective public health exists among all peoples" and "that's why the United States has strongly supported Taiwan's inclusion in efforts against SARS and beyond."

By the annual meeting of the WHA in 2005, Taiwan lamented that the United States did not speak up and that the WHO signed a Memorandum of Understanding (MOU) with the PRC to govern the WHO's technical exchanges with Taiwan.[46] Still, the Bush Administration "applauded" the WHO and China for taking steps in 2005 to greatly increase Taiwan's participation in WHO conferences.[47]

---

[46] In May 2007, the Formosan Association of Public Affairs (FAPA) released the "Implementation of the Memorandum of Understanding between the WHO Secretariat and China."

[47] Melody Chen, "Support for WHO Bid Dries Up," *Taipei Times*, May 18, 2005; State Department, "Taiwan: The World Health Assembly," May 19, 2006. In November 2005, Taiwan's Center for Disease Control participated in a (continued...)

In March 2007, the State Department submitted a required report to Congress on Taiwan's participation at the WHO, stating support for Taiwan's observership and opposition to its membership. The report noted demarches sent by the United States and other countries to the WHO to support expanded contacts with Taiwan.[48] In April 2007, the Administration also issued demarches to the WHO about political or nomenclature conditions placed on Taiwan's participation. In April 2007, Taiwan applied for membership in the WHO,[49] and the bid was rejected in May at the WHA by a vote of 17-148 (including U.S. opposition).

Taiwan did not gain observer status at the WHA in May 2008, even as the KMT's Ma Ying-jeou was inaugurated as President after Chen Shui-bian's terms ended. In January 2009, the WHO included Taiwan in the International Health Regulations (IHR) which entered into force in 2007. President Ma shifted Taiwan's focus to the WHA meeting (rather than the WHO). In its required report submitted to Congress on April 1, 2009, the State Department stated that it supported Taiwan's observership in the WHA and welcomed the decrease in politicization over Taiwan's participation in the WHO due to improvements in the cross-strait relationship over the past year. The State Department also asserted that U.S. efforts resulted in the attendance of Taiwan's experts in some technical meetings in 2005 and 2006. At the WHA in May 2009, Taiwan's Minister of Health participated for the first time as an observer.

However, some have concerns that the invitation required the PRC's approval, came under the WHO-PRC MOU, and was ad hoc (only for a KMT President). Indeed, the State Department's report to Congress in April 2010 acknowledged that the WHA invited Taiwan in 2009 after the PRC "agreed to Taiwan's participation." The State Department also expressed support, assessing that Taiwan's participation in the WHA was a "positive development" and could provide a model for Taiwan's participation as an "observer" in other U.N. bodies. In its report to Congress of April 2011, the State Department stated that it worked for Taiwan's observership at the WHA again in 2010 and has sought regular invitations from the WHO to Taiwan every year. However, in May 2011, a secret WHO Memorandum dated September 14, 2010, came to light, showing that the WHO had an "arrangement with China" to implement the IHR for the "Taiwan Province of China." That month in Geneva, Secretary of Health and Human Services Kathleen Sebelius protested to the WHO that no U.N. body has a right to determine unilaterally Taiwan's status.

Select Legislation (Enacted by Congress)

During the **103rd Congress**, the Congress passed and President Clinton signed (on April 30, 1994) the Foreign Relations Authorization Act for FY1994 and FY1995 (P.L. 103-236) that, inter alia, directed the State Department to register foreign-born Taiwanese-Americans as U.S. citizens born in Taiwan (rather than China); and called for the President to send Cabinet-level officials to Taiwan and to show clear U.S. support for Taiwan in bilateral and multilateral relationships.

After the Administration denied President Lee Teng-hui a visa in May 1994, the Senate, from July to October, passed amendments introduced by Senator Brown to ensure that Taiwan's President can enter the United States on certain occasions. Two amendments (for S. 2182 and H.R. 4606)

(...continued)

WHO conference on bird flu.

[48] State Department, "United States Support for Taiwan's Participation as an Observer at the 60th World Health Assembly and in the Work of the World Health Organization," 2007.

[49] Chen Shui-bian, "The Shunning of a State," *Washington Post*, May 11, 2007.

that passed were not retained, but the amendment to the Immigration and Nationality Technical Corrections Act of 1994 was enacted. Upon signing it into law (P.L. 103-416) on October 25, 1994, President Clinton said that he construed Section 221 as expressing Congress' view. Later, Congress overwhelmingly passed the bipartisan H.Con.Res. 53 expressing the sense of Congress that the President should promptly welcome a private visit by President Lee Teng-hui to his alma mater, Cornell University, and a transit stop in Anchorage, Alaska, to attend a conference. The House passed the resolution by 396-0 on May 2, and the Senate passed it by 97-1 on May 9, 1995 (with Senator Johnston voting Nay and Senators Moynihan and Warner not voting).

During the **106th Congress**, in 1999, Congress legislated a requirement for semi-annual reports on such U.S. support, in Section 704 of the Foreign Relations Authorization Act for FYs 2000 and 2001 (P.L. 106-113). Also in 1999, Congress passed legislation (P.L. 106-137) requiring a report by the Secretary of State on efforts to support Taiwan's participation in the WHO. In January 2000, the State Department submitted the report, saying that the United States does not support Taiwan's membership in organizations, such as the U.N. or WHO, where statehood is a requirement for membership, but that it supports any arrangements acceptable to the WHO membership to allow for Taiwan to participate in the work of the WHO.[50] In October 2000, the House and Senate passed H.Con.Res. 390, expressing the sense of Congress that the State Department's report failed to endorse Taiwan's participation in international organizations and that the United States should fulfill the commitment of the Taiwan Policy Review to more actively support Taiwan's participation in international organizations.

In the **107th Congress**, on May 17, 2001, Members in the House agreed without objection to H.Con.Res. 135 to welcome President Chen Shui-bian upon his visit.

Also, Congress enacted legislation, P.L. 107-10, authorizing the Secretary of State to initiate a U.S. plan to obtain observer status for Taiwan at the annual summit of the World Health Assembly in May 2001 in Geneva, Switzerland.[51] Then, Representative Sherrod Brown and Senator Torricelli introduced H.R. 2739 and S. 1932 to amend the law to target the May 2002 meeting. H.R. 2739 was passed and enacted as P.L. 107-158 on April 4, 2002.

As enacted on September 30, 2002, the Foreign Relations Authorization Act for FY2003 (**P.L. 107-228**), authorized—at the Bush Administration's request—U.S. departments or agencies (including the Departments of State and Defense) to assign or detail employees to the American Institute in Taiwan (AIT), the non-profit corporation (with offices in Washington and Taipei) that has handled the U.S.-Taiwan relationship in the absence of diplomatic ties since 1979 under the TRA. (Personnel at AIT were technically "separated" from government service for a period of time, raising issues about employment status, benefits, recruitment, etc.) The legislation also expressed the sense of Congress that AIT and the residence of its director in Taipei should publicly display the U.S. flag "in the same manner as United States embassies, consulates, and official residences throughout the world." AIT in Taipei has flown the U.S. flag only occasionally.

In the **108th Congress**, the House and Senate passed S. 243 to authorize the Secretary of State to initiate a U.S. plan to obtain observer status for Taiwan at the World Health Assembly in May 2003. Upon signing the bill as **P.L. 108-28** on May 29, 2003, President Bush stated that "the

---

[50] Department of State, "Report Required by P.L. 106-137, Fiscal Year 2000, Taiwan Participation in the World Health Organization (WHO)," January 4, 2000.

[51] The Vatican, Order of Malta, and Palestinian Liberation Organization (PLO) have observed the WHA's meetings.

United States fully supports the overall goal of Taiwan's participation in the work of the World Health Organization (WHO), including observership" but considered the act to be consistent with the "one China" policy. On October 30, 2003, the House passed H.Con.Res. 302 by 416-0 to welcome President Chen to the United States.

On April 21 and May 6, 2004, the House and Senate passed H.R. 4019 and S. 2092 in support of Taiwan's efforts to gain observer status in the WHO and to make it an **annual requirement** to have an unclassified report from the Secretary of State on the U.S. plan to help obtain that status for Taiwan. The implication of this change was the end of annual congressional statements and votes on this issue. In signing S. 2092 into law (**P.L. 108-235**) on June 14, 2004, President Bush stated that the United States fully supported the participation of Taiwan in the work of the WHO, including observer status. However, he also declared that his Administration shall construe the reporting requirement by using his authority to "withhold information" which could impair foreign relations or other duties of the Executive Branch.

Issue Area 2: Use of Force

The PRC has never renounced its claimed right to use force in what it sees as an internal problem and, moreover, has voiced more explicitly and demonstrated clearly its willingness to use force for political if not military objectives—despite its announced policy of "peaceful unification" since 1979. Since the early 1990s, the PRC has purchased more advanced arms from the Soviet Union/Russia and built up its theater missile force. In December 1992 and March 1993, PRC President Jiang Zemin and Premier Li Peng began to warn of having to use "drastic" or "resolute" measures to prevent Taiwan independence. In 1995-1996, the PRC launched provocative military exercises, including missile "test-firings," to express displeasure with then Taiwan President Lee Teng-hui's private visit to the United States and to intimidate voters before the first democratic presidential election in Taiwan. The United States believes that the PLA accelerated its buildup since the Taiwan Strait Crisis in 1995-1996. President Clinton deployed two aircraft carrier battle groups near Taiwan in March 1996. The PRC raised tension again in 1999, after KMT President Lee used the phrase of "special state-to-state ties" for the cross-strait relationship. President Bush did not support Taiwan's DPP President Chen Shui-bian (2000-2008) nor Taiwan's independence or membership in the U.N. and opposed referendums on membership in the U.N. for Taiwan during its presidential election on March 22, 2008. For that election, President Bush positioned two aircraft carriers near Taiwan, whose largely symbolic referendums were nonetheless targets of the PRC's belligerent condemnation. The referendums failed to be valid, and KMT candidate Ma Ying-jeou won as president.

Three Ifs

In February 2000, on the eve of another presidential election in Taiwan, the PRC issued its second White Paper on Taiwan, reaffirming the peaceful unification policy but adding a new precondition for the use of force. As one of "Three Ifs," the PRC officially warned that even if Taiwan indefinitely refuses to negotiate a peaceful settlement, the PRC would be compelled to use force to achieve unification. However, no deadline was issued. The White Paper also warned the United States not to sell arms to Taiwan or pursue any form of alliance with Taiwan, including cooperation in missile defense.

Commitment to Help Taiwan's Self-Defense

Since the 1950s, the United States government, with a critical congressional role, has expressed the consistent position for a peaceful resolution of the Taiwan question. Implementation of U.S. policy included the U.S.-ROC Defense Treaty of 1954 and the **Formosa Resolution, P.L. 84-4**.[52] After termination of the treaty, Congress passed and President Carter signed the TRA of 1979, adding U.S. commitment to assist Taiwan's self-defense and a potential U.S. role in maintaining peace in the strait. The TRA left the U.S. obligation to help defend Taiwan somewhat ambiguous and did not bind future U.S. decisions. Section 2(b)(4) states that the United States will consider with "grave concern" any non-peaceful means to determine Taiwan's future. The TRA also excluded the islands off the mainland (e.g., Quemoy and Matsu) in its security coverage over Taiwan. Nonetheless, the Section 2(b)(6) of the TRA declares it to be policy to maintain the U.S. capacity to resist any resort to force *or other forms of coercion* that would jeopardize the security, or the social or economic system, of the people on Taiwan [emphasis added].

In 1982, President Reagan signed the Joint Communique on reducing arms sales to Taiwan, but he also stated in public and internal clarifications that U.S. arms sales will continue in accordance with the TRA and with the full expectation that the PRC's approach to the resolution of the Taiwan issue will continue to be peaceful. President George H. W. Bush decided in September 1992 to sell 150 F-16 fighters to Taiwan, citing concerns about the cross-strait military balance.

On March 10 and 11, 1996, the Clinton Administration announced decisions to deploy two aircraft carrier battle groups to waters off Taiwan, after the PRC announced renewed PLA exercises that would include further missile "test-firings" toward Taiwan and Congress introduced legislation on helping to defend the ROC. President Clinton demonstrated that there might be grave consequences, as well as grave concern, to non-peaceful efforts to determine Taiwan's future. However, the Joint Statement at the 1997 Clinton-Jiang summit did not mention the TRA.

---

[52] Congress, in the 1950s, started to debate critical issues about whether to use U.S. military forces to defend the ROC government on the island of Taiwan, whether to include the small off-shore islands close to the mainland in any security coverage, and the role of Congress in such decision-making. After KMT forces, led by Chiang Kai-Shek, retreated to Taiwan in 1949, President Truman stated in January 1950 that the United States would not interfere in China's civil war to defend Taiwan. After North Korea's attack on South Korea in June 1950, however, Truman ordered the 7th Fleet to prevent attacks by both sides across the Taiwan Strait. In March 1953, the ROC asked for a mutual defense treaty, but the United States was concerned about extending any defense commitment to the off-shore islands, changing the "no-defense policy." PLA forces increased activities around the off-shore islands in mid-1953, seizing some small islands. In August 1954, Secretary of State John Foster Dulles announced that there would be a U.S.-ROC Mutual Defense Treaty (signed on December 2, 1954), and PRC bombardment and attacks on off-shore islands started the Taiwan Strait crisis of 1954-1955. (See Ralph Clough, *Island China*, Harvard University Press, 1978; Robert Accinelli, *Crisis and Commitment*, University of North Carolina Press, 1996.) On January 24, 1955, President Eisenhower, in a message to Congress, requested a resolution to authorize the use of force to protect Formosa, the Pescadores, and "related positions and territories." He said that he did not suggest that "the United States enlarge its defensive obligations beyond Formosa and the Pescadores as provided by the treaty now awaiting ratification." He also argued that it was important that Formosa remained in friendly hands and if in unfriendly hands, the situation would create a breach in the "island chain" of the western Pacific for U.S. and allied security. The President cited Communist firing of heavy artillery on Quemoy island that started in September 1954, followed by air attacks against the Tachen islands and seizure of Ichiang island. After significant debate, Congress passed H.J.Res. 159 on January 29, 1955. The Formosa Resolution was enacted as P.L. 84-4. The Senate Foreign Relations Subcommittee on U.S. Security Agreements and Commitments Abroad held extensive hearings on November 24, 25, 26, 1969, and May 8, 1970, to review "United States Security Agreements and Commitments Abroad with the Republic of China."

In April 2001, President George W. Bush publicly stated the U.S. commitment to Taiwan as an obligation to do "whatever it took to *help* Taiwan defend herself" [emphasis added].[53] Visiting two allies then China in February 2002, the President, in Tokyo, cited the U.S. commitment to Taiwan in the context of support for five regional allies (Japan, South Korea, Australia, Philippines, and Thailand)—to applause from the Diet, or Japan's legislature. Then, in Beijing, Bush emphasized U.S. commitments to the TRA and a peaceful settlement of the Taiwan question, while voicing opposition to provocations from either side.

However, indicating concerns about miscalculations of U.S. views in Taiwan, Deputy Assistant Secretary of Defense Richard Lawless told Taiwan's Deputy Defense Minister Chen Chao-min in February 2003 that, while the President said we will do whatever it takes to help Taiwan defend itself, Taiwan "should not view America's resolute commitment to peace and stability in the Taiwan Strait as a substitute for investing the necessary resources in its own defense."[54]

In November 2003, with concerns about PRC threats and Taiwan President Chen Shui-bian's efforts to hold referendums, Deputy Secretary of State Richard Armitage said that the TRA is not a defense treaty. Armitage added that the TRA guides policy in providing Taiwan "sufficient defense articles for her self-defense" and "also requires the United States to keep sufficient force in the Asia Pacific area to be able to keep the area calm." Armitage reaffirmed that the U.S. commitment to assist Taiwan's self-defense, with no defense treaty, "doesn't go beyond that in the Taiwan Relations Act, and we have good, competent military forces there."[55] President Bush appeared with PRC Premier Wen Jiabao in the Oval Office on December 9, 2003, and stated U.S. opposition to any unilateral decisions made by the leader of Taiwan to change the status quo.

In April 2004, Assistant Secretary of State James Kelly further clarified U.S. policy after Chen Shui-bian's re-election in March and warned Taiwan not to dismiss PRC statements as "empty threats" and warned of "limitations" to U.S. support for constitutional changes in Taiwan. At the same time, Assistant Secretary of Defense for International Security Affairs Peter Rodman warned Beijing that its attempt to use force would "inevitably" involve the United States.[56]

Aside from the issue of whether the U.S. strategy on assisting Taiwan's self-defense should be ambiguous or clear in a policy seeking deterrence towards Beijing and Taipei, a third view advocates the removal of any defense commitment (implicit or explicit) while continuing to sell weapons for Taiwan's self-defense.[57]

---

[53] Assessments differed on the implications of Bush's interpretation of the U.S. commitment. Congress expressed mixed reactions. Senator Joseph Biden wrote that "we now appear to have a policy of ambiguous strategic ambiguity. It is not an improvement." (*Washington Post*, May 2, 2001.) Senator Richard Lugar contended that the President's statement "reflected a common-sense appraisal of the strategic situation in Asia." (*Washington Times*, May 17, 2001.) The *Wall Street Journal* (April 26, 2001) wrote that Bush sent a message to Beijing that Washington has a "strong national interest in preserving Taiwan's democracy" and there is "now less chance of a miscalculation by China's leaders." Others, including Michael O'Hanlon (*New York Times*, April 27, 2001), said Bush departed from ambiguity, which serves U.S. interests in preserving all options and in discouraging provocations by Taipei. A third argument was that the U.S. defense commitment to Taiwan should be limited to arms sales and that "preserving Taiwan's de facto independence" is not a vital U.S. security interest (Ted Galen Carpenter, "Going Too Far: Bush's Pledge to Defend Taiwan," CATO Institute Foreign Policy Briefing, May 30, 2001).

[54] U.S.-Taiwan Business Council conference, San Antonio, TX, February 2003.

[55] Richard Armitage, press availability, Exhibit Hall, Washington, DC, November 18, 2003.

[56] Hearing on "The Taiwan Relations Act: The Next 25 Years," held by the House International Relations Committee, April 21, 2004.

[57] Ted Galen Carpenter (Cato Institute), *America's Coming War with China: A Collision Course over Taiwan*, 2005.

Arms Sales and Military Relationship

Despite the absence of diplomatic and alliance relations, U.S. arms sales to Taiwan have been significant. Moreover, beginning after tensions in the Taiwan Strait in 1995-1996, the Pentagon under the Clinton Administration quietly expanded the sensitive military relationship with Taiwan to levels unprecedented since 1979. These broader exchanges reportedly have increased attention to so-called "software," discussions over strategy, logistics, command and control, and plans in the event of an invasion of Taiwan.[58]

The George W. Bush Administration continued and expanded the closer military ties at different levels. In April 2001, President Bush announced he would drop the 20-year-old annual arms talks process used in relations with Taiwan's military in favor of normal, routine considerations of Taiwan's requests on an as-needed basis. Then, the Bush Administration granted a visa for ROC Defense Minister Tang Yiau-ming to visit the United States to attend a private conference held by the U.S.-Taiwan Business Council on March 10-12, 2002, in St. Petersburg, FL, making him the first ROC defense minister to come to the United States on a non-transit purpose since 1979.[59] Tang met with Deputy Secretary of Defense Paul Wolfowitz, who told the conference that the United States is willing to help Taiwan's military to strengthen civilian control, enhance jointness, and rationalize arms acquisitions.[60] In July 2002, the Pentagon issued a report to Congress on the PLA, warning that "the PRC's ambitious military modernization casts a cloud over its declared preference for resolving differences with Taiwan through peaceful means." The report also stressed that "Beijing has developed a range of non-lethal coercive options, including political/diplomatic, economic, and military measures."[61] The assessment has policy implications, since according to the TRA, it is U.S. policy to maintain the U.S. capacity to resist any resort to force or other forms of "coercion" against Taiwan's security, or social or economic system.

Also in 2002, the Bush Administration requested legislation be passed to authorize the assignment of personnel from U.S. departments and agencies to AIT, with implications for the assignment of active-duty military personnel to Taiwan for the first time since 1979. (See the discussion below of the Foreign Relations Authorization Act for FY2003.) While allowing military representatives in Taiwan, the Administration maintained a ban on visits by U.S. general and flag officers to Taiwan, under the State Department's "Guidelines on Relations with Taiwan."

Although there has been much interest among U.S. academic circles and think tanks in pursuing talks with China on its military buildup and increased U.S. security assistance to Taiwan,[62] a catalyst for this debate among policymakers arose out of the U.S.-PRC summit in Crawford, TX, on October 25, 2002. As confirmed to Taiwan's legislature by its envoy to Washington, C.J. Chen, and reported in Taiwan's media, PRC leader Jiang Zemin offered in vague terms a freeze or

---

[58] See CRS Report RL30957, *Taiwan: Major U.S. Arms Sales Since 1990*, by Shirley A. Kan.

[59] In December 2001, the previous ROC Defense Minister, Wu Shih-wen, made a U.S. transit on his way to the Dominican Republic.

[60] Deputy Secretary of Defense Paul Wolfowitz, "Remarks to the U.S.-Taiwan Business Council," March 11, 2002.

[61] Department of Defense, "Annual Report on the Military Power of the People's Republic of China," July 12, 2002.

[62] See David Lampton and Richard Daniel Ewing, "U.S.-China Relations in a Post-September 11th World," Nixon Center, August 2002; David Shambaugh's remarks at conference held by the Carnegie Endowment, Stanford University, Center for Strategic and International Studies, and National Committee on U.S.-China Relations, on "Taiwan and U.S. Policy: Toward Stability or Crisis?," October 9, 2002; Michael Swaine, "Reverse Course? The Fragile Turnaround in U.S.-China Relations," Carnegie Endowment Policy Brief, February 2003; and David Lampton, "The Stealth Normalization of U.S.-China Relations," *National Interest*, Fall 2003.

reduction in China's deployment of missiles targeted at Taiwan, in return for restraints in U.S. arms sales to Taiwan.[63] President Bush reportedly did not respond to Jiang's linkage. Policy considerations include the TRA (under which the United States has based its defense assistance to Taiwan on the threat that it faces), the 1982 Joint Communique (which discussed reductions in U.S. arms sales to Taiwan premised on the PRC's peaceful unification policy), and the 1982 "Six Assurances" to Taiwan (which said the United States did not agree to hold prior consultations with the PRC on U.S. arms sales to Taiwan). On April 21, 2004, Assistant Secretary of State James Kelly testified to the House International Relations Committee that if the PRC meets its stated obligations to pursue a peaceful resolution of the Taiwan issue and matches its rhetoric with a military posture that bolsters and supports peaceful approaches to Taiwan, "it follows logically that Taiwan's defense requirements will change."

Select Legislation (Enacted by Congress)[64]

Since the 1990s, particularly given the PLA's provocative exercises and missile launches in 1995 and 1996, Congress has asserted its role vis-a-vis the President in determining arms sales to Taiwan, as stipulated by Section 3(b) of the TRA, as well as in exercising its oversight of the TRA, including Section 2(b)(6) on the U.S. capacity to resist any resort to force or other forms of coercion against Taiwan.

During the **103rd Congress**, the Congress passed and President Clinton signed (on April 30, 1994) the Foreign Relations Authorization Act for FY1994 and FY1995 (P.L. 103-236) that, inter alia, declared that Sec. 3 of the TRA (i.e., on arms sales) takes primacy over policy statements (i.e., the 1982 joint communique).

During the **104th Congress**, in early 1996, Congress became increasingly concerned about provocative PLA exercises held the previous summer and again on the eve of Taiwan's presidential election in March 1996 (with "test-firings" of M-9 short-range ballistic missiles to target areas close to the two Taiwan ports of Kaohsiung and Keelung). Introduced by Representative Chris Cox on March 7, passed by the House on March 19, and passed by the Senate on March 21, 1996, H.Con.Res. 148 expressed the sense of Congress that the United States should assist in defending the ROC. On March 13, 1996, during markup of H.Con.Res. 148 in the House International Relations Subcommittee on Asia and the Pacific, Delegate Eni Faleomavaega noted that House and Senate resolutions prompted the Clinton Administration to deploy the USS Independence and USS Nimitz carriers. The resolution cited Section 3(c) of the TRA, which directs the President to inform Congress promptly of any threat to the security or the social or economic system of the people on Taiwan and to determine the U.S. response along with Congress. However, on March 14, 1996, Assistant Secretary of State for East Asian and Pacific Affairs Winston Lord told the Subcommittee that "however serious, the present situation does not constitute a threat to Taiwan of the magnitude contemplated by the drafters of the Taiwan Relations Act" and that "if warranted by circumstances, we will act under Section 3(c) of the TRA, in close consultation with the Congress."

In the **105th Congress**, the FY1999 National Defense Authorization Act (P.L. 105-261) required the Secretary of Defense to study the U.S. missile defense systems that could protect and could be transferred to "key regional allies," defined in the conference report as Japan, South Korea, and

---

[63] *Chung-Kuo Shih-Pao [China Times]*, November 22, 2002; *Taipei Times*, November 23, 2002.

[64] Also see CRS Report RL30957, *Taiwan: Major U.S. Arms Sales Since 1990*, by Shirley A. Kan.

Taiwan.[65] In addition, the conference report (H.Rept. 105-746 of the FY1999 Defense Appropriations Act, P.L. 105-262) required a report from the Pentagon on the security situation in the Taiwan Strait, in both classified and unclassified forms.[66]

In the **106th Congress**, the FY2000 National Defense Authorization Act (P.L. 106-65) enacted a requirement for the Pentagon to submit annual reports on PRC military power and the security situation in the Taiwan Strait.

In asserting its role in decision-making on arms sales to Taiwan, Congress passed language, introduced by Senator Lott, in the FY2000 Foreign Operations Appropriations Act (in Div. B of P.L. 106-113), requiring the Secretary of State to consult with Congress to devise a mechanism for congressional input in determining arms sales to Taiwan. Again, in the FY2001 Foreign Operations Appropriations Act (Sec. 581 of P.L. 106-429), Congress passed the Taiwan Reporting Requirement, requiring the President to consult on a classified basis with Congress 30 days prior to the next round of arms sales talks. (Those consultations took place on March 16, 2001.)

In addition to examining defense transfers to Taiwan, Congress also began to look closer at U.S. military deployments. The Consolidated Appropriations Act for FY2000 (P.L. 106-113) required a report on the operational planning of the Defense Department to implement the TRA and any gaps in knowledge about PRC capabilities and intentions affecting the military balance in the Taiwan Strait.[67]

In the **107th Congress**, the National Defense Authorization Act for FY2002 (P.L. 107-107), enacted December 28, 2001, authorized the President to transfer (by sale) the four Kidd-class destroyers to Taiwan (Sec. 1011), under Section 21 of the AECA. Also, Section 1221 of the act required a section in the annual report on PRC military power (as required by P.L. 106-65) to assess the PLA's military acquisitions and any implications for the security of the United States and its friends and allies. The scope of arms transfers to be covered was not limited to those from Russia and other former Soviet states, as in the original House language (H.R. 2586).[68]

The Foreign Operations Appropriations Act for FY2002 (P.L. 107-115), as enacted on January 10, 2002, brought unprecedented close coordination between the Executive and Legislative branches on arms sales to Taiwan. Section 573 required the Departments of State and Defense to provide detailed briefings (not specified as classified) to congressional committees (including those on appropriations) within 90 days of enactment and not later than every 120 days thereafter during FY2002. The briefings were to report on U.S.-Taiwan discussions on potential sales of defense articles or services.

Some Members in the House and Senate called for ensuring regular and high-level consultations with Taiwan and a role for Congress in determining arms sales to Taiwan, after President Bush

---

[65] Department of Defense, "Report to Congress on Theater Missile Defense Architecture Options for the Asia-Pacific Region," May 1999; CRS Report RL30379, *Missile Defense Options for Japan, South Korea, and Taiwan: A Review of the Defense Department Report to Congress*, by Robert D. Shuey, Shirley A. Kan, and Mark Christofferson.

[66] Department of Defense, "Report to Congress Pursuant to the FY99 Appropriations Bill, The Security Situation in the Taiwan Strait," February 1, 1999; CRS Report RS20187, *Taiwan's Defense: Assessing The U.S. Department of Defense Report, "The Security Situation in the Taiwan Strait"*, by Robert G. Sutter.

[67] Department of Defense, "Report to Congress on Implementation of the Taiwan Relations Act," December 2000.

[68] Still, the Pentagon's report, issued on July 12, 2002, discussed China's military acquisitions from states of the former Soviet Union, and not other countries (e.g., Israel).

announced on April 24, 2001, that he would drop the annual arms talks process with Taiwan in favor of normal, routine considerations on an "as-needed" basis. Enacted as P.L. 107-228, the Foreign Relations Authorization Act for FY2003 authorized—at the Bush Administration's request—the Department of State and other departments or agencies (including the Department of Defense) to detail employees to AIT (Section 326); required that Taiwan be "treated as though it were designated a major non-NATO ally" (Section 1206); required consultations with Congress on U.S. security assistance to Taiwan every 180 days (Section 1263); and authorized the sale to Taiwan of the four Kidd-class destroyers (Section 1701). Section 326, amending the Foreign Service Act of 1980, has significant implications for the assignment of government officials to Taiwan, including active-duty military personnel for the first time since 1979.

In signing the bill into law on September 30, 2002, President Bush issued a statement that included his view of Section 1206 (on a "major non-NATO ally"). He said that "Section 1206 could be misconstrued to imply a change in the 'one China' policy of the United States when, in fact, that U.S. policy remains unchanged. To the extent that this section could be read to purport to change United States policy, it impermissibly interferes with the President's constitutional authority to conduct the Nation's foreign affairs." Nonetheless, the Acting Under Secretary of Defense for Acquisition, Technology, and Logistics, Michael Wynne, submitted a letter to Congress on August 29, 2003, that designated Taiwan as a "major non-NATO ally."

The House-passed FY2003 National Defense Authorization Act contained Section 1202 seeking to require the Secretary of Defense to implement a comprehensive plan to conduct combined training and exchanges of senior officers with Taiwan's military and to "enhance interoperability" with Taiwan's military. The language was similar to that of Section 5(b) in the Taiwan Security Enhancement Act proposed in the 106th Congress. The Senate's version did not have the language. As enacted on December 2, 2002, the legislation (P.L. 107-314) contains a revised section (1210) requiring a Presidential report 180 days after the act's enactment on the feasibility and advisability of conducting combined operational training and exchanges of senior officers with Taiwan's military. (Military exchanges may take place in the United States, but U.S. flag/general officers may not visit Taiwan.)[69]

In the **110th Congress**, the House Foreign Affairs Committee approved, on September 26, 2007, H.Res. 676 (introduced by Representative Ileana Ros-Lehtinen) that noted the Bush Administration's lack of response to Taiwan's interest in buying F-16C/D fighters and that urged the Administration to determine security assistance "based solely" upon the legitimate defense needs of Taiwan (citing Section 3(b) of the TRA). The House passed H.Res. 676 on October 2, 2007. The House also passed H.R. 6646 on September 23, 2008. Some Members suspected that Bush had a "freeze" on arms sales to Taiwan until notifications to Congress on October 3, 2008.

In the **111th Congress**, Senator John Cornyn introduced on July 23, 2009, an amendment to the National Defense Authorization Act for FY2010 to require President Obama to report on an assessment of Taiwan's air force, in examining Taiwan's need for new F-16C/D fighters. In conference, the Senate Armed Services Committee receded on the section to require in the legislation for a Presidential report on Taiwan's air force and U.S. options. Nonetheless, the conference report (H.Rept. 111-288) directed the Defense Secretary to submit an unclassified report to Congress on an assessment of Taiwan's air defense. The bill was enacted as P.L. 111-84 on October 28, 2009, and Secretary Gates submitted a study to Congress in February 2010.

---

[69] Department of State, "Guidelines on Relations with Taiwan," memo, February 2, 2001.

Issue Area 3: Dialogue

President Nixon in 1972, President Carter in 1978, and President Reagan in 1982 publicly stated the U.S. expectation that the Chinese themselves will settle the Taiwan question. President Reagan also gave "Six Assurances" to Taiwan in 1982. The assurances to Taipei, made just before the United States and the PRC issued the August 17, 1982 Joint communique, included assurances that Washington will not mediate between Taipei and Beijing, and will not pressure Taipei to negotiate with Beijing.

Urging Cross-Strait Dialogue

One policy question concerns the extent of U.S. encouragement of cross-strait dialogue and the U.S. role in any talks or negotiations to resolve the Taiwan question. As Taipei and Beijing's economic relationship grew to significant levels by the early 1990s and the two sides began to talk directly through quasi-official organizations, the Clinton Administration increasingly voiced its support for the cross-strait dialogue, encouraging Taipei in particular. Like a bystander, the State Department said in its Taiwan Policy Review of 1994 that "the United States applauds the continuing progress in the cross-strait dialogue." After talks broke off and military tensions flared, however, the Administration, after 1996, privately and publicly urged both sides to hold this dialogue as an added part of a more proactive U.S. policy. In July 1996, National Security Advisor Anthony Lake visited China and planned a meeting (later canceled) with Wang Daohan, head of the PRC's organization for cross-strait talks. At the 1997 U.S.-PRC summit, President Clinton urged for a peaceful resolution "as soon as possible" and that "sooner is better than later."

In March 1999, Assistant Secretary of State Stan Roth raised the possibility of "interim agreements" between Beijing and Taipei, after several prominent former Clinton Administration officials made similar proposals. Roth's mention of possible "interim agreements" raised concerns in Taipei that it was a proposal by the Clinton Administration to pressure Taipei into negotiating with Beijing. Roth's remarks came in the context of suggestions to reduce cross-strait tensions issued by former or future Clinton Administration officials. In January 1998, a delegation of former officials led by former Defense Secretary William Perry had visited Beijing and Taipei, reportedly passing a message from the PRC that it was willing to resume talks with Taiwan. The February 21, 1998 *Washington Post* reported that the delegation was part of the Administration's effort to have a "track two" dialogue with Beijing and Taipei and to encourage resumption of cross-strait talks. At a February 1998 conference in Taipei, Kenneth Lieberthal (a University of Michigan professor who later joined the NSC as the Senior Director for Asian Affairs in August 1998) had proposed a 50-year "interim arrangement" in which the PRC (as "China") would renounce the use of force against Taiwan, and the ROC (as "Taiwan, China") would agree not to declare independence (*Reuters*, March 1, 1998).

In the March 8, 1998 *Washington Post*, Joseph Nye (former Assistant Secretary of Defense for International Security Affairs) had proposed a "three-part package" that would include a clarification that Washington would not recognize or defend Taiwan independence but also would not accept the use of force against Taiwan, and a "one country, three systems" approach. Also in March 1998, former National Security Advisor Anthony Lake had visited Taiwan and reportedly encouraged resumption of cross-strait talks. In *Foreign Affairs* (July/August 1998), Chas. Freeman (former Assistant Secretary of Defense for International Security Affairs) had urged Washington to encourage Beijing and Washington to defer negotiations on their long-term relationship for a certain period, such as 50 years, and to reevaluate arms sales to Taiwan. In February-March 1999, Perry had led another delegation, including retired Admiral Joseph

Prueher (later nominated in September 1999 to be ambassador to Beijing), and the group made suggestions to the PRC and Taiwan on how to reduce cross-strait tensions, according to *Notes from the National Committee* (Winter/Spring 1999). Later, on September 5, 1999, Deputy Assistant Secretary of State Susan Shirk mentioned "one country, three systems" as a possible approach for "one China," Taiwan media reported.

In contrast to this stress on dialogue, the George W. Bush Administration started by emphasizing deterrence and approved Taiwan's requests for major arms in 2001. In 2004, National Security Advisor Condoleezza Rice did urge Beijing to resume cross-strait talks and offered a vague U.S. role "to further dialogue if it is helpful."[70] Though the Administration repeatedly stated that Beijing should talk to the duly-elected leaders in Taipei, the Administration continued the approach of non-mediation in any talks by those two parties. In 2005, in answer to Representative Leach about a U.S. role as "facilitator," Deputy Assistant Secretary of State Randall Schriver vaguely responded that good U.S. relations with Beijing and Taipei allow Washington to "assist the two sides in getting to the negotiating table on mutually agreeable terms."[71]

Lamenting a "graveyard of missed opportunities" in cross-strait ties, a former Chairman of AIT, Richard Bush, thoroughly assessed this question of possible U.S. roles and concluded that greater U.S. involvement to encourage direct dialogue makes sense and that the role should be limited to "intellectual facilitation" to clarify policy stances and objectives of each side. Ken Lieberthal called again for U.S. encouragement of cross-strait negotiation for an agreed framework.[72]

Three Pillars and "Assent" of Taiwan's People

In July 1999, the Clinton Administration's stance on cross-strait dialogue culminated in the President's articulation of a new phrase: that U.S. policy has "three pillars" (one China, peaceful resolution, and cross-strait dialogue). Recognizing Taiwan's newly established status as a democracy, however, President Clinton in February 2000 added the U.S. expectation that the cross-strait dispute be resolved not only peacefully but also "with the assent" of Taiwan's people.

Bush Administration's Re-emphasis of the "Six Assurances"

The George W. Bush Administration began after Chen Shui-bian of the DPP became ROC President in May 2000. The Bush Administration indicated that it would not pressure Taipei to hold cross-strait dialogue, re-emphasizing the "Six Assurances" given to Taipei by President Reagan in 1982. At a hearing in March 2001, Secretary of State Colin Powell assured Senator Jesse Helms that the "Six Assurances" remained U.S. policy and that the Administration would not favor consulting the PRC on arms sales to Taiwan.[73] On June 12, 2001, Assistant Secretary of State James Kelly testified to the House International Relations Subcommittee on East Asia and the Pacific that U.S. defensive arms sales to Taiwan make a peaceful cross-strait resolution more likely. He said that "the central question is how cross-strait relations can move from a focus on

---

[70] Philip Pan, "Rice Rebuffs China on Taiwan Arms Sales," *Washington Post*, July 9, 2004.

[71] Responses for the record of a hearing on China's "Anti-Secession Law" and developments across the Taiwan Strait held by the House International Relations Subcommittee on Asia and the Pacific, April 6, 2005.

[72] Richard Bush, *Untying the Knot: Making Peace in the Taiwan Strait*, Brookings Institution: 2005; Kenneth Lieberthal, Professor at University of Michigan, "Preventing a War Over Taiwan," *Foreign Affairs*, March/April 2005.

[73] Senate Foreign Relations Committee, Hearing on U.S. Foreign Policy, March 8, 2001.

the military balance toward a focus on ways to begin resolving differences between Taipei and Beijing." While calling for a resumption of direct dialogue, economic cooperation, and mutual understanding, Kelly also said that "the PRC cannot ignore the elected representatives of the people of Taiwan." While visiting Taiwan at about the same time that PRC Vice Premier Qian Qichen signaled a new receptive policy toward the ruling DPP in Taiwan, Richard Bush, Chairman of AIT, said on January 28, 2002, that "the United States favors and encourages dialogue but has no intention of serving as a mediator in this dispute or of pressuring Taiwan to negotiate." He added that "it does not seem constructive for one side to set pre-conditions for a resumption of dialogue that the other side even suspects would be tantamount to conceding a fundamental issue before discussion begins."

In March 2002, Assistant Secretary of State Kelly told attendees at a conference that the Bush Administration would continue to uphold the "Six Assurances," meaning no U.S. mediation and no pressure on Taiwan to go to the bargaining table.[74] In testimony at a hearing in April 2004, after Chen Shui-bian's re-election in the March election, Kelly again reaffirmed the "Six Assurances," but explicitly warned that "a secure and self-confident Taiwan is a Taiwan that is more capable of engaging in political interaction and dialogue with the PRC, and we expect Taiwan will not interpret our support as a blank check to resist such dialogue." He urged both Beijing and Taipei to pursue dialogue "as soon as possible" and "without preconditions."[75]

Obama Administration and Convergence on "Peaceful Development"

In 2005, the KMT and CPC agreed on a party-to-party platform of cross-strait "peaceful development." After the KMT's Ma Ying-jeou became president in Taiwan in 2008, CPC General Secretary Hu Jintao issued a policy toward Taiwan of "peaceful development." After President Obama took office, he held a summit in Beijing in November 2009 with Hu Jintao, and they issued the first U.S.-PRC Joint Statement in 12 years since the Clinton-Jiang Joint Statement of 1997. In the 2009 Joint Statement, the United States declared that it welcomed the "peaceful development" of relations across the Taiwan Strait and looked forward to efforts by both sides to increase dialogues and interactions in economic, political, and other fields, and develop more positive and stable cross-strait relations. Nonetheless, AIT Chairman Ray Burghardt clarified at a news conference in Taipei on November 24, 2009, that the Joint Statement should not be interpreted as putting pressure on Taiwan to negotiate with the PRC.

Select Legislation (Enacted by Congress)

As enacted on September 30, 2002, the Foreign Relations Authorization Act for FY2003 (P.L. 107-228), reaffirmed President Clinton's February 2000 condition for settling Taiwan's status and expressed the sense of Congress that any resolution of the Taiwan question must be peaceful and "include the assent of the people of Taiwan."

---

[74] U.S.-Taiwan Business Council, defense industry conference, St. Petersburg, FL, March 10-12, 2002.

[75] House International Relations Committee, "The Taiwan Relations Act: The Next 25 Years," April 21, 2004.

Overview of Policy Issues

In short, since 1971, U.S. Presidents—both secretly and publicly—have continued to articulate a "one China" *policy* in understandings with the PRC. Nonetheless, policymakers have continued to face unresolved issues, while the political and strategic context of the policy has changed dramatically since the early 1970s. Congressional oversight of successive Presidents has watched for any new agreements with Beijing and any shift in the U.S. stance closer to that of Beijing's "one China" *principle*—on questions of sovereignty, arms sales, or dialogue. Since the 1990s, successive Administrations also have shown more explicit opposition—through arms sales, force deployments, deeper U.S.-Taiwan military ties, and public statements—to PRC efforts to use force or coercion to determine Taiwan's future. Not recognizing the PRC's claim over Taiwan or Taiwan as a sovereign state, U.S. policy has considered Taiwan's status as unsettled. U.S. policy leaves the Taiwan question to be resolved by the people on both sides of the strait: a "peaceful resolution" with the assent of Taiwan's people and without unilateral changes. In other words, U.S. policy focuses on the *process* of resolution of the Taiwan question, not any set outcome.

This approach, however, encounters challenges from Taiwan as it denies being an ambiguous non-entity and asserts a sovereign status, as the ROC under the KMT or Taiwan under the DPP. Even as the United States has opposed a unilateral change from Beijing or Taipei to the status quo, the meaning of "status quo" remains a question. Some say that instead of a "status quo," the situation in the Taiwan Strait has changed significantly, including the shifting military balance to favor the PRC and the rapid rapprochement and extensive engagement—beyond détente— between the PRC and Taiwan under the CPC and KMT's dialogues, particularly since 2008.

There has been no comprehensive review of U.S. policy since 1994. Some said that a U.S. strategy or a policy review might be needed to seek positive objectives and sustain U.S. security, political, and economic interests with Taiwan or with the PRC.[76] For a hearing on January 13, 2009, on Hillary Clinton's confirmation to be Secretary of State, the Senate Foreign Relations Committee asked a question for the record about whether the Administration would hold another Taiwan Policy Review, but she did not answer the question. Still, Admiral Robert Willard, Commander of the Pacific Commander (PACOM) in Honolulu, initiated in January 2010 reviews of approaches toward the PRC and toward Taiwan (among other concerns like North Korea) by "Strategic Focus Groups (SFGs)," narrower efforts than a review by the Obama Administration.

In any examination of U.S. policy or strategy, whether through recalibrations or review, Congress and the Administration face critical issues under the rubric of the "one China" policy, including:

---

[76] See Randall Schriver, "Taiwan Needs Six New Assurances," *Taipei Times*, August 22, 2007, and "In Search of a Strategy," *Taiwan Business Topics*, American Chamber of Commerce-Taipei, September 2007. On a debate over whether a policy review is needed, particularly after the KMT's Ma Ying-jeou became president in May 2008, and whether to reduce or strengthen the relationship with Taiwan, see Robert Sutter, "Cross-Strait Moderation and the United States—Policy Adjustments Needed," PacNet Newsletter #17, March 5, 2009; and Richard Bush and Alan Romberg, "Cross-Strait Moderation and the United States – A Response to Robert Sutter," PacNet Newsletter #17A, March 12, 2009 (Pacific Forum CSIS); Robert Sutter, "Taiwan's Future: Narrowing Straits," NBR Analysis, May 2011; controversial academic articles with a theme of abandoning Taiwan in *Foreign Affairs* by Bruce Gilley, "Not So Dire Straits: How the Finlandization of Taiwan Benefits U.S. Security," January/February 2010; responses in May/June 2010; Charles Glaser, "Will China's Rise Lead to War? Why Realism Does Not Mean Pessimism," March/April 2011; and a response by Daniel Blumenthal, "Rethinking U.S. Foreign Policy Towards Taiwan," *Foreign Policy*'s Shadow Government blog, March 2, 2011; Joseph Prueher, Charles Freeman III, Timothy Keating, David Michael Lampton, James Shinn, et al., "A Way Ahead with China," University of Virginia, January 2011.

- How are internal as well as cross-strait political, economic, and military trends serving or undermining U.S. interests and leverage over Beijing and Taipei?

- What are the implications for U.S. interests and policies of the significant engagement (including the CPC-KMT cooperation) across the Taiwan Strait, particularly since May 2008?

- What are likely outcomes (e.g., unsettled status, unification, independence, confederation, commonwealth), and what are impacts on U.S. interests?

- What are the implications of strategies conducted by Beijing and Taipei?

- Are policy elements of diplomacy and deterrence balanced?

- Should Washington change any assurances or positions?

- Should U.S. policy positions (support, non-support, opposition) be clarified to deter provocations from Beijing or Taipei (e.g., on use of force or coercion, Taipei's moves toward de jure independence)?

- Should the United States proactively deepen its role (e.g., facilitation, mediation) to encourage cross-strait negotiation and/or appoint a special envoy/coordinator?

- How should defense policies (on arms sales, military cooperation, U.S. force deployments, missile defense) be carried out to increase U.S. leverage in Taiwan, deter conflict, and counter coercion?

- What is the extent of the U.S. commitment to help Taiwan's self-defense?

- How might the United States be more supportive of Taiwan in its preservation of international space—distinct from the PRC?

- How well are U.S. policies coordinated with those of our allies, including European countries in NATO, Japan, South Korea, and Australia?

Part II: Highlights of Key Statements by Washington, Beijing, and Taipei

In Part II below, this CRS Report provides excerpts from key statements on "one China" as articulated by Washington, Beijing, and Taipei, in addition to the three Joint Communiques and the TRA, since the United States first reached understandings with the PRC in 1971.[77] Based on unclassified sources and interviews, the highlights also give a comprehensive look at significant statements and contexts in Washington, Beijing, as well as Taipei. This compilation identifies new, major (not all) elements in the policies of the governments. The statements also include accounts of presidential assurances. The three perspectives on "one China" are placed in chronological order under successive U.S. Administrations. The texts are placed in italics.

---

[77] Following the ROC government's retreat to Taiwan in 1949 and the start of the Korean War, the U.S. stance shifted on sovereignty over Taiwan. On January 5, 1950, President Truman stated that the United States would not get involved in the civil conflict in China. After the Korean War started, however, President Truman declared on June 27, 1950, that "the determination of the future status of Formosa must await the restoration of security in the Pacific, a peace settlement with Japan, or consideration by the United Nations." (Quoted by Alan Romberg, *Rein in at the Brink of the Precipice*, Stimson Center, 2003).

Statements During Nixon Administration

Kissinger's Secret Talks with PRC Premier Zhou Enlai[78]

July 9, 1971

Our military presence in Taiwan at this moment is composed of two elements, the two-thirds of it which is related to activities in other parts of Asia [the Vietnam War] and the one-third of it which is related to the defense of Taiwan. We are prepared to remove that part related to activities other than to the defense of Taiwan, that's two-thirds of our force ... within a specified brief period of time after the ending of the war in Indochina. We are prepared to begin reducing our other forces on Taiwan as our relations improve, so that the military questions need not be a principal obstacle between us. I may say, incidentally, that these are personal decisions of President Nixon which have not yet been discussed with our bureaucracy or with Congress, and so should be treated with great confidence.

As for the political future of Taiwan, we are not advocating a "two Chinas" solution or a "one China, one Taiwan" solution.

[On Zhou Enlai's question of whether the United States would support the Taiwan independence movement]: *We would not support this.*

Nixon's "Five Principles" in Secret Talks with Zhou Enlai

February 22, 1972[79]

Principle one. There is one China, and Taiwan is a part of China. There will be no more statements made—if I can control our bureaucracy—to the effect that the status of Taiwan is undetermined.

Second, we have not and will not support any Taiwan independence movement.

---

[78] Holdridge, John, *Crossing the Divide: An Insider's Account of Normalization of U.S.-China Relations* (Rowman & Littlefield Publishers, 1997), p. 90. See also: James Mann, *About Face: A History of America's Curious Relationship with China, From Nixon to Clinton* (New York: Alfred A. Knopf, 1999), p. 33 (citing a declassified chronology from the Central Intelligence Agency (CIA) by Richard Solomon, *U.S.-PRC Political Negotiations, 1967-84, An Annotated Chronology*, December 1985, released to Mann (a *Los Angeles Times* reporter) under the Freedom of Information Act). Mann reports that what Kissinger pledged to Zhou went beyond previous U.S. promises and contradicted the official U.S. position that sovereignty over Taiwan was "an unsettled question subject to future international resolution." At a Senate Foreign Relations Committee hearing on March 25, 1999, Assistant Secretary of State Stanley Roth also cited Kissinger's promise as recorded in the CIA's chronology in his written response to Senator Helms' question about precedents for President Clinton's June 1998 "Three Noes" statement. Also see Patrick Tyler, *A Great Wall* (New York: PublicAffairs, 1999), p. 98. On February 27, 2002, the National Security Archive released declassified copies of U.S. documents on U.S.-PRC rapprochement in 1970-1971, including transcripts of National Security Adviser Henry Kissinger's secret meetings in China. Quotations are from the White House Memorandum, dated July 29, 1971, written by Winston Lord for Kissinger on his conversations with Zhou on July 9.

[79] White House, Memorandum of Conversation, February 22, 1972, 2:10pm-6:00pm. On December 11, 2003, the National Security Archive, an organization in Washington, DC, was able to release the declassified Top Secret Memoranda of Conversation on President Nixon's meetings in Beijing in February 1972, which led to the Shanghai Communique. On the American side, only President Nixon, National Security Advisor Henry Kissinger, and two NSC staff, John Holdridge and Winston Lord, were in the meetings.

Third, we will, to the extent we are able, use our influence to discourage Japan from moving into Taiwan as our presence becomes less, and also discourage Japan from supporting a Taiwan independence movement. I will only say here I cannot say what Japan will do, but so long as the U.S. has influence with Japan—we have in this respect the same interests as the Prime Minister's government—we do not want Japan moving in on Taiwan and will discourage Japan from doing so.

The fourth point is that we will support any peaceful resolution of the Taiwan issue that can be worked out. And related to that point, we will not support any military attempts by the Government on Taiwan to resort to a military return to the Mainland.

Finally, we seek the normalization of relations with the People's Republic. We know that the issue of Taiwan is a barrier to complete normalization, but within the framework I have previously described, we seek normalization and we will work toward that goal and will try to achieve it.

Nixon on Withdrawing U.S. Military Forces from Taiwan

February 24, 1972[80]

With regard to Taiwan, I do not believe a permanent American presence—whatever happens in our meetings—is necessary to American security.... My goal is the withdrawal of our remaining forces, not just two-thirds, but all forces, including the remaining one-third.... It must be consistent with ... the so-called Nixon Doctrine. Under that Doctrine, we are cutting our forces in Korea.... Two-thirds will go, hopefully as soon as we can finish our Vietnam involvement. My plan also is one which reduces the one-third and withdraws it during the period I have the power to act. But I cannot do it before January of next year. It has to be over a period of four years. Now if someone asks me when I return, do you have a deal with the Prime Minister that you are going to withdraw all American forces from Taiwan, I will say "no." But I am telling the Prime Minister that it is my plan.... [81]

U.S.-PRC Joint Communique (Shanghai Communique)

February 27, 1972

The Chinese reaffirmed its position: The Taiwan question is the crucial question obstructing the normalization of relations between China and the United States; the Government of the People's Republic of China is the sole legal government of China; Taiwan is a province of China which has long been returned to the motherland; the liberation of Taiwan is China's internal affair in which no other country has the right to interfere; and all U.S. forces and military installations must be withdrawn from Taiwan. The Chinese Government firmly opposes any activities which aim at the creation of "one China, one Taiwan," "one China, two governments," "two Chinas," and "independent Taiwan" or advocate that "the status of Taiwan remains to be determined."

---

[80] White House, Memorandum of Conversation, February 24, 1972, 5:15pm-8:05pm, classified as Top Secret until release as declassified documents on December 11, 2003.

[81] As part of his response, Zhou Enlai remarked to Nixon that "you hope for and will not hinder a peaceful liberation [of Taiwan]." Nixon did not correct Zhou.

The U.S. side declared: The United States acknowledges[82] that all Chinese on either side of the Taiwan Strait[83] maintain there is but one China and that Taiwan is a part of China. The United States Government does not challenge that position. It reaffirms its interest in a peaceful settlement of the Taiwan question by the Chinese themselves. With this prospect in mind, it affirms the ultimate objective of the withdrawal of all U.S. forces and military installations from Taiwan. In the meantime, it will progressively reduce its forces and military installations on Taiwan as the tension in the area diminishes.

Mao Zedong on Use of Force[84]

November 12, 1973

As for the question of our relations with Taiwan, that is quite complex. I do not believe in a peaceful transition.... They are a bunch of counter-revolutionaries [the Nationalists on Taiwan]. How could they cooperate with us? I say that we can do without Taiwan for the time being, and let it come after "100 years."

Statements During Ford Administration

President Ford's Address to a Joint Session of Congress[85]

August 12, 1974

To the People's Republic of China, whose legendary hospitality I enjoyed, I pledge continuity in our commitment to the principles of the Shanghai communique. The new relationship built on those principles has demonstrated that it serves serious and objective mutual interests and has become an enduring feature of the world scene.

---

[82] The Chinese text used *"ren shi"* ("to acknowledge"). The Chinese term was changed in the 1979 communique to "recognize."

[83] Holdridge (p. 89), then a senior staff member for East Asia at the National Security Council under Henry Kissinger, wrote that "it was helpful that both the CCP [Chinese Communist Party] and the Kuomintang [(KMT) or Nationalist Party] regarded Taiwan as part of China, for by accepting this point and affirming our interest in the settlement of the sovereignty question 'by the Chinese themselves' we would affront neither side." Holdridge (p. 93) also recounted that the wording of "all Chinese" was originally formulated as "all people," and the State Department objected to the word "people," because some on Taiwan regarded themselves as "Taiwanese" and did not agree that Taiwan was a part of China.

[84] Tyler, p. 172, citing Henry Kissinger, Memorandum of Conversation with Mao Zedong, Chairman Mao's residence, November 12, 1973. One year later, in a meeting with Deng Xiaoping in Beijing, Tyler writes that Kissinger stated his understanding that Mao had said that the leadership would ultimately have to solve the Taiwan question by force and it could take 100 years. Deng said that "100 years" was symbolic. Kissinger was concerned about a military solution to the Taiwan question shortly after U.S.-PRC normalization.

[85] *Public Papers of the Presidents, Gerald Ford, 1974.*

Statements During Carter Administration

U.S. Statement on Diplomatic Recognition of the PRC[86]

December 15, 1978

As of January 1, 1979, the United States of America recognizes the People's Republic of China as the sole legal government of China.

In the future, the American people and the people of Taiwan will maintain commercial, cultural and other relations without official government representation and without diplomatic relations. The Administration will seek adjustments to our laws and regulations to permit the maintenance of commercial, cultural, and other non-governmental relationships in the new circumstances that will exist after normalization. The United States is confident that the people of Taiwan face a peaceful and prosperous future. The United States continues to have an interest in the peaceful resolution of the Taiwan issue and expects that the Taiwan issue will be settled peacefully by the Chinese themselves.[87]

PRC Statement on Establishing China-U.S. Diplomatic Relations[88]

December 16, 1978

As is known to all, the Government of the People's Republic of China is the sole legal government of China and Taiwan is a part of China. The question of Taiwan was the crucial issue obstructing the normalization of relations between China and the United States. It has now been resolved between the two countries in the spirit of the Shanghai Communique and through their joint efforts, thus enabling the normalization of relations so ardently desired by the people of the two countries. As for the way of bringing Taiwan back to the embrace of the motherland and reunifying the country, it is entirely China's internal affair.

---

[86] In great secrecy, the Carter White House made its final decision to normalize relations with the PRC. President Carter, along with National Security Advisor Zbigniew Brzezinski and his aide, Michel Oksenberg, did not consult with Congress on the timing and final wording of the communique. Congress was surprised to be informed hours before the December 15, 1978 announcement. See Patrick Tyler, "The (Ab)normalization of U.S.-Chinese Relations," *Foreign Affairs*, September/October 1999; Cyrus Vance, *Hard Choices* (New York: Simon and Schuster, 1983); Robert G. Sutter (CRS), "Executive-Legislative Consultations on China Policy, 1978-79," Foreign Affairs Committee Print, June 1980. In a speech at Stanford University in honor of Michel Oksenberg on May 6, 2002, Carter said he became president in 1977 determined to establish full diplomatic relations with China. He said he kept negotiations instructions to his envoy, Leonard Woodcock, secret from the State Department, and only Secretary of State Cyrus Vance went to the White House, which sent direct communications to Woodcock.

[87] President Carter announced the new policy, despite the International Security Assistance Act (P.L. 95-384) enacted on September 26, 1978. Congress passed it with Senator Robert Dole's amendment, saying that it is the sense of Congress that it be consulted on any proposed policy changes affecting the U.S.-ROC Mutual Defense Treaty. Senator Jacob Javits later wrote that the President made his announcement "with only the briefest notice to congressional leaders," and regarding the abrogation of the defense treaty, "the President's action ignored a specific amendment adopted by the Congress only two months before, in the International Security Assistance Act of 1978, calling for 'prior consultation' on 'any proposed policy changes affecting the continuation in force' of that treaty." ("Congress and Foreign Relations: the Taiwan Relations Act," *Foreign Affairs*, Fall 1981).

[88] "Statement of the Government of the People's Republic of China in Connection with the Establishment of China-U.S. Diplomatic Relations," printed in Harding.

ROC President Chiang Ching-kuo's Statement[89]

December 29, 1978

The Republic of China is an independent sovereign state with a legitimately established government based on the Constitution of the Republic of China. It is an effective government, which has the wholehearted support of her people. The international status and personality of the Republic of China cannot be changed merely because of the recognition of the Chinese Communist regime by any country of the world. The legal status and international personality of the Republic of China is a simple reality which the United States must recognize and respect.

PRC's New Year's Message to Compatriots in Taiwan[90]

January 1, 1979

Taiwan has been an inalienable part of China since ancient times.... Taiwan's separation from the motherland for nearly 30 years has been artificial and against our national interests and aspirations, and this state of affairs must not be allowed to continue....

Unification of China now fits in with the direction of popular feeling and the general trend of development. The world in general recognizes only one China, with the Government of the People's Republic of China as the sole legal government. The recent conclusion of the China-Japan Treaty of Peace and Friendship and the normalization of relations between China and the United States show still more clearly that no one can stop this trend....

We place great hopes on the 17 million people on Taiwan and also the Taiwan authorities. The Taiwan authorities have always taken a firm stand of one China and opposed an independent Taiwan. This is our common stand and the basis for our cooperation....

The Chinese Government has ordered the People's Liberation Army [PLA] to stop the bombardment of Quemoy and other islands as of today. A state of military confrontation between the two sides still exists along the Taiwan Strait. This can only create artificial tension. We hold that first of all this military confrontation should be ended through discussion between the Government of the People's Republic of China and the Taiwan authorities so as to create the necessary prerequisites and a secure environment for the two sides to make contacts and exchanges in whatever area....

---

[89] "President Chiang Ching-kuo's Five Principles on U.S.-ROC Relations in the Post-Normalization Period," December 29, 1978, printed in Martin L. Lasater, *The Taiwan Issue in Sino-American Strategic Relations* (Boulder: Westview Press, 1984). Lasater notes that Chiang informed U.S. Deputy Secretary of State Warren Christopher that future U.S.-ROC ties must rest on five underlying principles of reality, continuity, security, legality, and governmentality. The statement was summarized by James Soong, Deputy-Director of the ROC's Government Information Office.

[90] "Text of NPC Standing Committee Message to Taiwan Compatriots," *New China News Agency*, December 31, 1978. This policy of "unification" replaced the earlier one of "liberation" of Taiwan. The PRC later elaborated on this policy of peaceful unification in Marshal Ye Jianying's "Nine-Point Proposal" of September 30, 1981.

U.S.-PRC Joint Communique on the Establishment of Diplomatic Relations (Normalization Communique)

January 1, 1979

The United States of America recognizes the Government of the People's Republic of China as the sole legal Government of China. Within this context, the people of the United States will maintain cultural, commercial, and other unofficial relations with the people of Taiwan.

The Government of the United States of America acknowledges[91] the Chinese[92] position that there is but one China and Taiwan is part of China.

Taiwan Relations Act (TRA), P.L. 96-8

Enacted April 10, 1979

Section 2(b) It is the policy of the United States

(1) to preserve and promote extensive, close, and friendly commercial, cultural, and other relations between the people of the United States and the people on Taiwan, as well as the people on the China mainland and all other peoples of the Western Pacific area;[93]

(2) to declare that peace and stability in the area are in the political, security, and economic interests of the United States, and are matters of international concern;

(3) to make clear that the United States decision to establish diplomatic relations with the People's Republic of China rests upon the expectation that the future of Taiwan will be determined by peaceful means;

(4) to consider any effort to determine the future of Taiwan by other than peaceful means, including by boycotts or embargoes, a threat to the peace and security of the Western Pacific area and of grave concern to the United States;[94]

---

[91] In the Chinese text, the word for "acknowledge" is "*cheng ren*" (recognize), a change from "*ren shi*" (acknowledge), used in the 1972 Shanghai Communique. During debate on the TRA in February 1979, Senator Jacob Javits noted the difference and said that "it is very important that we not subscribe to [the Chinese position on one China] either way." Deputy Secretary of State Warren Christopher responded that "we regard the English text as being the binding text. We regard the word 'acknowledge' as being the word that is determinative for the U.S." (Wolff and Simon, p. 310-311).

[92] Instead of the phrase "all Chinese on either side of the Taiwan Strait" in the 1972 Shanghai communique, the 1979 Normalization communique used "the Chinese position" (in the English text) and "China's position" (in the Chinese text).

[93] A key issue for Congress was to consider the character of the relationship with Taiwan. While the "Normalization Communique" and the Administration called for "unofficial" U.S. relations with Taiwan, Members objected to the use of that word. Congress omitted any adjective for the relationship and AIT, and the TRA does not specify the relationship as official or unofficial. In discussing the legislative history of the unprecedented law, Senator Jacob Javits wrote that "no one really knew what the limits of 'officiality' were." ("Congress and Foreign Relations: the Taiwan Relations Act," *Foreign Affairs*, Fall 1981).

[94] On this language in the TRA, the House report and statements of key Members of Congress (such as Rep. Zablocki, chairman of the House Foreign Affairs Committee) clarified the expectation that there would be a "prompt response" by the United States to a use of force against Taiwan, but the TRA would not specify in advance what the situation or response might be. Members also stated the expectation that the President would promptly inform Congress of
(continued...)

---

(5) to provide Taiwan with arms of a defensive character; and

(6) to maintain the capacity of the United States to resist any resort to force or other forms of coercion that would jeopardize the security, or the social or economic system, of the people on Taiwan.[95]

Sec. 3(a) In furtherance of the policy set forth in section 2 of this Act, the United States will make available to Taiwan such defense articles and defense services in such quantity as may be necessary to enable Taiwan to maintain a sufficient self-defense capability.

(b) The President and the Congress shall determine the nature and quantity of such defense articles and services based solely upon their judgment of the needs of Taiwan, in accordance with procedures established by law. Such determination of Taiwan's defense needs shall include review by United States military authorities in connection with recommendations to the President and the Congress.

(c) The President is directed to inform the Congress promptly of any threat to the security or the social or economic system of the people on Taiwan and any danger to the interests of the United States arising therefrom. The President and the Congress shall determine, in accordance with constitutional processes, appropriate action by the United States in response to any such danger.

Sec. 4(b)(1) Whenever the laws of the United States refer or relate to foreign countries, nations, states, governments, or similar entities, such terms shall include and such laws shall apply with respect to Taiwan.[96]

Sec. 15(2) The term "Taiwan" includes, as the context may require, the islands of Taiwan and the Pescadores,[97] *the people on those islands, corporations and other entities and associations*

(...continued)

anticipated dangers to Taiwan, and the President and the Congress would both determine the appropriate U.S. response according to the Constitution. Some Members, such as Rep. Dodd, considered the language on "grave concern" to be "strong" and "unambiguous," but Rep. Quayle noted that "of grave concern" is a "very ambiguous term we read every day in the newspapers." Thus, he added language that became section 2(b)(6) of the TRA. (Wolff and Simon, p. 77-91).

[95] Senator Jacob Javits wrote that Members of Congress debated the appropriate characterization of U.S. concern for Taiwan's security. Congress "did not seek to reconstruct a defense agreement with Taiwan," and majorities in the House and Senate agreed with the Administration in opposing Senator Charles Percy's amendment to characterize "coercion" against Taiwan as a threat to the "security interests" of the United States, because such language would "unnecessarily convey an intention to reenact the security agreement itself, thus violating one of the understandings with Beijing." Nonetheless, Javits wrote that Congress legislated a broad definition of the threats that Taiwan could face, going beyond language for resisting "armed attacks" generally put into defense treaties. He was "particularly concerned with other dangers which in fact seemed more realistic than an outright invasion from across the straits." ("Congress and Foreign Relations: the Taiwan Relations Act," *Foreign Affairs*, Fall 1981).

[96] According to an author of the language, Section 4(B)(1) treats Taiwan as a state for purposes limited to domestic U.S. laws (not international law), and without it, the United States could not sell Taiwan weapons or enriched uranium for nuclear power reactors, for example. (Author's consultation with Harvey Feldman, who wrote "President Reagan's Six Assurances to Taiwan and Their Meaning Today," Heritage Foundation, October 2, 2007.)

[97] Congress considered the security implications for the United States of whether the definition of "Taiwan" includes the offshore islands of Quemoy and Matsu (only a few miles off the mainland). The House report (p. 16) on the TRA noted that the definitions are "illustrative, not limiting." Nonetheless, Rep. Zablocki (chairman of the House Foreign Affairs Committee) explained that his committee excluded Quemoy and Matsu from the definition. He noted that these islands had been "deliberately left out of the mutual defense treaty," and "we should not be expanding the U.S. security commitment beyond what was in the treaty." He noted that "Quemoy and Matsu are considered by both Taipei and by Peking to be part of mainland China." He concluded that "as far as the reference in the committee report is concerned, (continued...)

---

created or organized under the laws applied on those islands, and the governing authorities on Taiwan recognized by the United States as the Republic of China prior to January 1, 1979, and any successor governing authorities (including political subdivisions, agencies, and instrumentalities thereof).[98]

Statements During Reagan Administration

PRC Leader Ye Jianying's Nine-Point Proposal[99]

September 30, 1981

Now, I would take this opportunity to elaborate on the policy concerning the return of Taiwan to the motherland for the realization of peaceful unification [proclaimed on New Year's Day 1979]:

1. *In order to bring an end to the unfortunate separation of the Chinese nation as early as possible, we propose that talks be held between the Communist Party of China and the Kuomintang [Nationalist Party] of China on a reciprocal basis so that the two parties will cooperate for the third time to accomplish the great cause of national unification. The two sides may first send people to meet for an exhaustive exchange of views.*

2. *It is the urgent desire of the people of all nationalities on both sides of the strait to communicate with each other, reunite with their relatives, develop trade and increase mutual understanding. We propose that the two sides make arrangements to facilitate the exchange of mail, trade, air and shipping services, and visits by relatives and tourists as well as academic, cultural, and sports exchanges, and reach an agreement thereupon.*

3. *After the country is reunified, Taiwan can enjoy a high degree of autonomy as a special administration region, and it can retain its armed forces. The central government will not interfere with local affairs in Taiwan.*

4. *Taiwan's current socio-economic system will remain unchanged, so will its way of life and its economic and cultural relations with foreign countries. There will be no encroachment on the proprietary rights and lawful right of inheritance over private property, houses, land and enterprises, or on foreign investments.*

(...continued)

it does not extend our security commitment in its referral to Quemoy and Matsu." (Wolff and Simon, p. 282-283.)

[98] On the legislative history of the TRA, see also commentaries by Representative Dante Fascell and Senators Alan Cranston, John Glenn, Jesse Helms, Richard Lugar, John McCain, and Claiborne Pell, in William Bader and Jeffrey Bergner (editors), *The Taiwan Relations Act: A Decade of Implementation*, Hudson Institute and SRI International, 1989. Bader was the Chief of Staff of the Senate Foreign Relations Committee in 1978-1981. See also: William Bader, "U.S. Has Law That Governs Relations with Taiwan," *Financial Times*, April 7, 2011.

[99] "Ye Jianying Explains Policy Concerning Return of Taiwan to Motherland and Peaceful Unification," *Xinhua [New China News Agency]*, September 30, 1981, in *FBIS*. According to the Chinese report, Ye spoke as the Chairman of the Standing Committee of the National People's Congress (the PRC's legislature). However, Ye enjoyed significant stature in the Chinese leadership largely because he was a Marshal, the highest rank in the PLA. Harding (p. 113, 155) wrote that Chinese Premier Zhao Ziyang later described the plan to President Reagan at a meeting in Cancun in October 1981, seeking reductions in and an end to U.S. arms sales to Taiwan.

---

5. *People in authority and representative personages of various circles in Taiwan may take up posts of leadership in national political bodies and participate in running the state.*

6. *When Taiwan's local finance is in difficulty, the central government may subsidize it as is fit for the circumstances.*

7. *For people of all nationalities and public figures of various circles in Taiwan who wish to come and settle on the mainland, it is guaranteed that proper arrangements will be made for them, that there will be no discrimination against them, and that they will have the freedom of entry and exit.*

8. *Industrialists and businessmen in Taiwan are welcome to invest and engage in various economic undertakings on the mainland, and their legal rights, interests, and profits are guaranteed.*

9. *The unification of the motherland is the responsibility of all Chinese. We sincerely welcome people of all nationalities, public figures of all circles, and all mass organizations in Taiwan to make proposals and suggestions regarding affairs of state through various channels and in various ways.*

Taiwan's return to the embrace of the motherland and the accomplishment of the great cause of national unification is a great and glorious mission history has bequeathed on our generation.... We hope that the Kuomintang authorities will stick to their one-China position and their opposition to "two Chinas" and that they will put national interests above everything else, forget previous ill will and join hands with us in accomplishing the great cause of national unification and the great goal of making China prosperous and strong, so as to win glory for our ancestors, bring benefit to our posterity, and write a new and glorious page in the history of the Chinese nation!

Letter from President Reagan to Deng Xiaoping[100]

April 5, 1982

Clearly, the Taiwan issue had been a most difficult problem between our governments.... The United States firmly adheres to the positions agreed upon in the Joint Communique on the establishment of diplomatic relations between the United States and China. There is only one China. We will not permit the unofficial relations between the American people and the people of Taiwan to weaken our commitment to this principle.

---

[100] Printed in Lasater.

Reagan's "Six Assurances" to Taiwan[101]

July 14, 1982

In negotiating the third Joint Communique with the PRC, the United States:

1. has not agreed to set a date for ending arms sales to Taiwan;

2. has not agreed to hold prior consultations with the PRC on arms sales to Taiwan;

3. will not play any mediation role between Taipei and Beijing;

4. has not agreed to revise the Taiwan Relations Act;

5. has not altered its position regarding sovereignty over Taiwan;

6. will not exert pressure on Taiwan to negotiate with the PRC.

Message from President Reagan to Taiwan President[102]

July 26, 1982

I want to point out that this decision [on a joint communique] is based on a PRC decision only to use peaceful means to resolve the Taiwan issue. On this point, the U.S. will not only pay attention to what the PRC says, but also will use all methods to achieve surveillance of PRC military production and military deployment. The intelligence attained would be brought to your attention. If there is any change with regard to their commitment to peaceful solution of the Taiwan issue, the U.S. commitments would become invalidated.

---

[101] "ROC Statement on the August 17 Communique," August 17, 1982. A slightly different version of the Six Assurances was reported by Steve Lohr, "Taiwan Expresses Regret Over Communique," *New York Times*, August 18, 1982. Also see Alan Romberg, *Rein In At the Brink of the Precipice* (Stimson Center, 2003). James Lilley, as Director of AIT, conveyed the Six Assurances in the form of a blind memo with no letterhead or signature to President Chiang Ching-kuo through ROC Vice Foreign Minister Fredrick Chien, who translated them from English to a Chinese text. Lilley explained that the Six Assurances were a sign to Taiwan that it was not being abandoned by the Reagan Administration. (James Lilley, *China Hands*, Public Affairs, 2004.) Chien wrote his translated Chinese version in *Chien Fu's Memoirs, Volume II* (Taipei, 2005). He wrote the fifth assurance as "the United States cannot support the PRC's position regarding sovereignty over Taiwan." Also: author's consultation with a U.S. official, June 2007.

[102] Feldman, Harvey, "Reagan's Commitment to Taiwan: the Real Meaning of the Taiwan Communique," *Washington Times*, April 24, 2001; "Taiwan, Arms Sales, and the Reagan Assurances," *American Asian Review*, Fall 2001. According to Feldman, James Lilley, Director of AIT, delivered a "non-paper" from President Reagan to ROC President Chiang Ching-kuo, which included this clarification of U.S. commitments. Lilley delivered this message in addition to the "Six Assurances" given on July 14, 1982. Feldman noted to CRS that he obtained the wording from Chien Fu, then the ROC's Vice Foreign Minister, who translated from a Chinese translation of an English text.

U.S.-PRC Joint Communique on Arms Sales (1982 Communique)[103]

August 17, 1982[104]

In the Joint Communique on the Establishment of Diplomatic Relations on January 1, 1979, issued by the Government of the United States of America and the Government of the People's Republic of China, the United States of America recognized the Government of the People's Republic of China as the sole legal government of China, and it acknowledged the Chinese position[105] that there is but one China and Taiwan is part of China.

The question of United States arms sales to Taiwan was not settled in the course of negotiations between the two countries on establishing diplomatic relations.

The Chinese government reiterates that the question of Taiwan is China's internal affair. The Message to the Compatriots in Taiwan issued by China on January 1, 1979, promulgated a fundamental policy of striving for peaceful unification of the Motherland. The Nine-Point Proposal put forward by China on September 30, 1981 represented a further major effort under this fundamental policy to strive for a peaceful solution to the Taiwan question.

The United States Government attaches great importance to its relations with China, and reiterates that it has no intention of infringing on Chinese sovereignty and territorial integrity, or interfering in China's internal affairs, or pursuing a policy of "two Chinas" or "one China, one Taiwan."[106] The United States Government understands and appreciates the Chinese policy of striving for a peaceful resolution of the Taiwan question as indicated in China's Message to Compatriots in Taiwan issued on January 1, 1979 and the Nine-Point Proposal put forward by China on September 30, 1981. The new situation which has emerged with regard to the Taiwan

---

[103] *Public Papers of the Presidents of the United States, Ronald Reagan*. Also, in *The Reagan Diaries* (published in 2007), President Reagan wrote in his entry for August 17, 1982, that "Press and TV with a leak from State Dept. has gone crazy declaring our joint communique with P.R.C. of China is a betrayal of Taiwan. Truth is we are standing with Taiwan and the P.R.C. made all the concessions." Earlier, on January 11, 1982, Reagan had written in his diary that "press running wild with talk that I reversed myself on Taiwan because we're only selling them F5Es & F104s [fighters]. I think the China Lobby in State Dept. is selling this line to appease the PRC which doesn't want us to sell them anything. The planes we're offering are better than anything the PRC has. Later on if more sophistication is needed we'll upgrade & sell them F5Gs."

[104] The Senate Judiciary Subcommittee on Separation of Powers held hearings on September 17 and 27, 1982, and subsequently communicated with the State Department to investigate "apparent conflicts" between the Reagan Administration's 1982 Communique and the TRA, and to seek clarifications on policy toward Taiwan from Secretary of State George Shultz. He answered that "a determination of Taiwan's defense needs and of the sufficiency of its self-defense capability requires an assessment of the nature of the military threat confronting it. This necessarily requires an assessment of the military capacity of the PRC and its policy towards Taiwan." Among extensive responses, Shultz also replied that U.S. arms sales do not violate China's sovereignty; that the United States takes no position on the question of Taiwan's sovereignty; and that the communique is not an international agreement. Lawyers for the Departments of State and Justice testified that the August 17, 1982 communique "sets forth parallel and interrelated statements of policy by the United States and China." Moreover, they stated that "it is not an international agreement and thus imposes no obligations on either party under international law. Its status under domestic law is that of a statement by the President of the United States of a policy which he intends to pursue. Like any other Presidential policy, it must be executed in full compliance with all relevant laws."

[105] The Chinese text says that the United States "recognized" ("*cheng ren*") "China's" ("*zhongguo de*") position, repeating the formulation of the 1979 communique.

[106] In response to a question at the Senate Foreign Relations Committee hearing of March 25, 1999, Assistant Secretary of State Stanley Roth cited this phrase as a precedent for President Clinton's June 1998 statement in China that the United States does not support Taiwan independence, as part of the "Three Noes."

---

question also provides favorable conditions for the settlement of United States-China differences over the question of United States arms sales to Taiwan.

Having in mind the foregoing statements of both sides, the United States Government states that it does not seek to carry out a long-term policy of arms sales to Taiwan, that its arms sales to Taiwan will not exceed, either in qualitative or in quantitative terms, the level of those supplied in recent years since the establishment of diplomatic relations between the United States and China, and that it intends to reduce gradually its sales of arms to Taiwan, leading over a period of time to a final resolution. In so stating, the United States acknowledges China's consistent position regarding the thorough settlement of this issue.[107]

President Reagan's Statement on U.S. Arms Sales to Taiwan[108]

August 17, 1982

Regarding future U.S. arms sales to Taiwan, our policy, set forth clearly in the communique [issued on the same day], is fully consistent with the Taiwan Relations Act. Arms sales will continue in accordance with the act and with the full expectation that the approach of the Chinese Government to the resolution of the Taiwan issue will continue to be peaceful. We attach great significance to the Chinese statement in the communique regarding China's "fundamental" policy, and it is clear from our statements that our future actions will be conducted with this peaceful policy fully in mind. The position of the United States Government has always been clear and consistent in this regard. The Taiwan question is a matter for the Chinese people, on both sides of the Taiwan Strait, to resolve. We will not interfere in this matter or prejudice the free choice of, or put pressure on, the people of Taiwan in this matter. At the same time, we have an abiding interest and concern that any resolution be peaceful. I shall never waver from this fundamental position.

Reagan's Secret Memorandum on the 1982 Communique[109]

August 17, 1982

---

[107] U.S. arms sales to Taiwan was an unresolved issue. James Lilley wrote that President Reagan refused to end arms sales, while he agreed to concede a limit on such sales. The final wording vaguely referred to a "final resolution" of the issue. (See James Lilley, *China Hands*, Public Affairs: 2004.) Later, Congress passed the Foreign Relations Authorization Act for FY1994 and FY1995 (P.L. 103-236, enacted on April 30, 1994), affirming that Sec. 3 of the TRA (on arms sales) takes primacy over policy statements (1982 Joint Communique), among other stipulations.

[108] "Statement on United States Arms Sales to Taiwan," August 17, 1982, *Public Papers of the Presidents of the United States, Ronald Reagan.*

[109] First publicly disclosed by James Mann, in *About Face* (Alfred Knopf, 1999). According to Mann, President Reagan's secret memorandum (on the August 17, 1982 communique) clarified U.S. policy as maintaining the military balance between the PRC and Taiwan. A version of the text, as provided by an unnamed former U.S. official, was published in Robert Kaiser, "What We Said, What They Said, What's Unsaid," *Washington Post*, April 15, 2001. According to Alan Romberg's *Rein In at the Brink of the Precipice* (Stimson Center, 2003), Charles Hill, then Executive Secretary of the State Department, confirmed that Secretary of State George Shultz was told by President Reagan that his intention was to solidify the stress on a peaceful resolution and the importance of maintaining the cross-strait military balance for that objective. Reagan also intended his written clarification to reassure Republicans in Congress, such as Senator Jesse Helms, that Taiwan would not be disadvantaged by the communique. Partial text of the memo was published by James Lilley, in *China Hands* (Public Affairs, 2004). Also, author's consultation with Lilley.

The U.S. willingness to reduce its arms sales to Taiwan is conditioned absolutely upon the continued commitment of China to the peaceful solution of the Taiwan-PRC differences. It should be clearly understood that the linkage between these two matters is a permanent imperative of U.S. foreign policy. In addition, it is essential that the quantity and quality of the arms provided Taiwan be conditioned entirely on the threat posed by the PRC. Both in quantitative and qualitative terms, Taiwan's defense capability relative to that of the PRC will be maintained.

PRC's Statement on the Communique[110]

August 17, 1982

In the joint communique, the Chinese Government reiterates in clear-cut terms its position that "the question of Taiwan is China's internal affair." The U.S. side also indicates that it has no intention of infringing on Chinese sovereignty and territorial integrity, or interfering in China's internal affairs, or pursuing a policy of "two Chinas" or "one China, one Taiwan."

Assistant Secretary of State Holdridge and "Six Assurances"[111]

August 18, 1982

*[On the August 17, 1982, communique], let me recapitulate and emphasize a few key features; then I'll take your questions. First, **the document must be read as a whole**, since the policies it sets forth are interrelated [original emphasis].*

*Second, as I have previously noted, the communique **contains a strong Chinese statement that its fundamental policy is to seek to resolve the Taiwan question by peaceful means** (Para 4) [original emphasis]....*

*Third, the **U.S. statements concerning future arms sales to Taiwan (Para 6) are based on China's statements** as to its fundamental peaceful policy for seeking a resolution to the Taiwan question and on the "new situation" created by those statements (Para 5) [original emphasis]....*

*Fourth, **we did not agree to set a date certain for ending arms sales to Taiwan** and the statements of future U.S. arms sales policy embodied in the Communique do not provide either a time frame for reductions of U.S. arms sales or for their termination....**We see no mediation role for the U.S. nor will we attempt to exert pressure on Taiwan to enter into negotiations with the PRC**.... There has been **no change in our long-standing position on the issue of sovereignty over Taiwan**. The communique (Para 1) in its opening paragraph simply cites that portion of the joint communique on the establishment of diplomatic relations between the U.S. and the P.R.C. in which the U.S. "acknowledged the Chinese position on this issue" (i.e., that there is but one*

---

[110] Harding.

[111] U.S. House, Committee on Foreign Affairs, Hearing on China-Taiwan: United States Policy, "Prepared Statement of John H. Holdridge, Assistant Secretary of State for East Asian and Pacific Affairs," August 18, 1982. On July 15, 1998, Assistant Secretary of State Stanley Roth submitted answers to questions posed at a hearing of the Senate Foreign Relations Committee on May 14, 1998, concerning "U.S. Interests at the June U.S.-China Summit." Roth responded to Senator Craig Thomas' question on abiding by the "Six Assurances" by stating a reaffirmation of the Administration's "commitment to the principles articulated by then-Assistant Secretary Holdridge in his 1982 testimony to the House Foreign Affairs Committee."

*China and Taiwan is a part of China).... It has been reported in the press that **the Chinese at one point suggested that the Taiwan Relations Act be revised. We have no plans to seek any such revisions**.... [Para 9] should not be read to imply that we have agreed to engage in prior consultations with Beijing on arms sales to Taiwan. [original emphasis]*

PRC Leader Deng Xiaoping on "One China, Two Systems"[112]

February 22, 1984

There are many disputes in the world that always require solutions. I have had the belief for many years that, no matter what solutions are used to solve these problems, don't use means of war, but use peaceful ways. Our proposal for unification between the mainland and Taiwan is fair and reasonable. After unification, Taiwan will still be allowed to engage in its capitalism, while the mainland implements socialism, but there will be one unified China. One China, two systems. The Hong Kong problem will also be treated the same: one China, two systems.[113]

Deng Xiaoping on Use of Force and Unification in "1,000 Years"[114]

June 22, 1984

If we cannot resolve peacefully [the Hong Kong and Taiwan questions], then can only use force to resolve, but this would be disadvantageous to all sides. Achieving national unification is the nation's wish, if not unified in 100 years, then unified in 1,000 years. In how to resolve this problem, I think it would only be through "one country, two systems."

Deng Xiaoping on "Peaceful Coexistence" and Taiwan's Military[115]

October 31, 1984

We proposed "one country, two systems" to resolve the problem of national unification, and that is a kind of peaceful coexistence. We resolved the Hong Kong problem, permitting Hong Kong to preserve the capitalist system with no change for 50 years. This principle also applies to the

---

[112] Deng's talk on "A New Way to Stabilize the World Situation," translated from *Deng Xiaoping Lun Guofang He Jundui Jianshe* [Deng Xiaoping Discusses National Defense and Military Construction], Junshi Kexue Chubanshe [Military Science Press], May 1992. During PRC-British talks on the future of Hong Kong, Deng conveyed his proposal for a "one country, two systems" formula in a meeting with former U.S. National Security Advisor Zbigniew Brzezinski, who visited China as part of a delegation from Georgetown University's Center for Strategic and International Studies. The meeting and Deng's decision of "effecting two systems within one country" was reported in *Wen Wei Po* (a PRC newspaper in Hong Kong), February 24, 1984; translated in *FBIS*, February 28, 1984. Deng's formula has been often translated as "one country, two systems," rather than the original "one China, two systems." Deng's remarks were also published in Chinese in *Deng Xiaoping's Selected Works.*

[113] Mann (p. 153-154) writes that after the conclusion of negotiations over Hong Kong, Deng launched a secret, intensive effort to settle with the Reagan Administration on the future of Taiwan. When British Prime Minister Margaret Thatcher signed the Hong Kong agreement in December 1984, Deng passed a message through her to Reagan, asking that the same formula of "one country, two systems" be applied to Taiwan. However, the message was not conveyed, but some Americans lobbied for the proposal. In the end, the Administration decided not to settle on Taiwan's future.

[114] Deng's remarks in Chinese published in *Deng Xiaoping's Selected Works.*

[115] Deng's remarks in Chinese published in *Deng Xiaoping's Selected Works.*

---

*Taiwan problem. Taiwan differs from Hong Kong and would be able to keep its military. ...
Taiwan could keep its capitalism, and Beijing would not assign people to Taiwan.*

Statements During George H. W. Bush Administration

Toast at the Welcoming Banquet in Beijing[116]

February 25, 1989

*We remain firmly committed to the principles set forth in those three joint communiques that form
the basis of our relationship. And based on the bedrock principle that there is but one China, we
have found ways to address Taiwan constructively without rancor. We Americans have a long,
historical friendship with Chinese people everywhere. In the last few years, we've seen an
encouraging expansion of family contacts and travel and indirect trade and other forms of
peaceful interchange across the Taiwan Strait, reflecting the interests of the Chinese people
themselves. And this trend, this new environment, is consistent with America's present and
longstanding interest in a peaceful resolution of the differences by the Chinese themselves.*

Taiwan's National Unification Guidelines; Policy on the PRC[117]

March 14, 1991

*[Unification is] to establish a democratic, free, and equitably prosperous China.... It should be
achieved in gradual phases under the principles of reason, peace, parity, and reciprocity.... [In
the short term,] to enhance understanding through exchanges between the two sides of the Strait
and eliminate hostility through reciprocity; and to establish a mutually benign relationship by not
endangering each other's security and stability while in the midst of exchanges and not denying
the other's existence as a political entity while in the midst of effecting reciprocity.*

Taiwan on the Meaning of "One China"[118]

August 1, 1992

*Both sides of the Taiwan Strait agree that there is only one China. However, the two sides of the
Strait have different opinions as to the meaning of "one China." To Peking, "one China" means
the "People's Republic of China (PRC)," with Taiwan to become a "Special Administration*

---

[116] *Public Papers of the Presidents, George Bush.*

[117] Text published in: Mainland Affairs Council, Executive Yuan, Republic of China, "Consensus Formed at the
National Development Conference on Cross-Strait Relations," February 1997. The Guidelines were adopted by the
National Unification Council on February 23, 1991, and by the Executive Yuan (Cabinet) on March 14, 1991. These
guidelines asserted the principle of "one China, two political entities," recognized the PRC's jurisdiction over the
mainland, and called for eventual unification on the basis of "parity" between the two sides. Then, on May 1, 1991,
Taiwan terminated the 1948 National Mobilization for Suppression of the Communist Rebellion, thus ending the civil
war against the Communists and recognizing the political authority of the PRC on the mainland.

[118] Text published in: Mainland Affairs Council, Executive Yuan, Republic of China, "Consensus Formed at the
National Development Conference on Cross-Strait Relations," February 1997. "The Meaning of 'One China'" was
adopted by the National Unification Council.

Region" after unification. Taipei, on the other hand, considers "one China" to mean the Republic of China (ROC), founded in 1911 and with de jure sovereignty over all of China. The ROC, however, currently has jurisdiction only over Taiwan, Penghu, Kinmen, and Matsu. Taiwan is part of China, and the Chinese mainland is part of China as well.

President Bush on the Sale of F-16s to Taiwan[119]

September 2, 1992

I'm announcing this afternoon that I will authorize the sale to Taiwan of 150 F-16A/B aircraft, made right here in Fort Worth.... This sale of F-16s to Taiwan will help maintain peace and stability in an area of great concern to us, the Asia-Pacific region, in conformity with our law. In the last few years, after decades of confrontation, great strides have been made in reducing tensions between Taipei and Beijing. During this period, the United States has provided Taiwan with sufficient defensive capabilities to sustain the confidence it needs to reduce those tensions. That same sense of security has underpinned Taiwan's dramatic evolution toward democracy.

My decision today does not change the commitment of this Administration and its predecessors to the three communiques with the People's Republic of China. We keep our word: our one-China policy, our recognition of the PRC as the sole legitimate government of China. I've always stressed that the importance of the 1982 communique on arms sales to Taiwan lies in its promotion of common political goals: peace and stability in the area through mutual restraint.

---

[119] Remarks to General Dynamics Employees in Fort Worth, Texas, September 2, 1992, *Administration of George Bush, 1992 (Public Papers of the Presidents)*. In addition to this arms sale decision, the Bush Administration also broke new ground in high-level exchanges with Taiwan. In Taiwan from November 30-December 3, 1992, U.S. Trade Representative Carla Hills was the first U.S. cabinet official to visit since de-recognition in 1979.

"One China, Different Interpretations" ("1992 Consensus")[120]

November 3, 1992

Taipei's SEF: *On November 3, a responsible person of the Communist Chinese ARATS said that it is willing to "respect and accept" SEF's proposal that each side "verbally states" its respective principles on "one China."*[121]

Beijing's ARATS: *At this working-level consultation in Hong Kong, SEF representatives suggested that each side use respective verbal announcements to state the one China principle. On November 3rd, SEF sent a letter, formally notifying that "each side will make respective statements through verbal announcements." ARATS fully respects and accepts SEF's suggestion.*[122]

---

[120] Beijing's Association for Relations Across the Taiwan Strait (ARATS) and Taipei's Strait Exchange Foundation (SEF) met in Hong Kong, October 28-30, 1992. Through these quasi-official organizations, the two sides agreed to disagree on the meaning of "one China," namely, "PRC" in Beijing and "ROC" in Taipei. However, years later, it became a semantic dispute. The CPC in Beijing and KMT in Taipei have argued that the two sides reached a "1992 Consensus," re-phrased by KMT official Su Chi for more ambiguity. The DPP has disagreed. On August 28, 2001, AIT Director Raymond Burghardt said that the two sides had exchanged faxes which constituted an agreement to hold talks, adding "I'm not sure why you could call that a consensus. I call it an agreement." In his National Day address of October 10, 2004, Chen suggested that the "1992 meeting" be the basis to resume cross-strait dialogue. On March 26, 2008, according to National Security Advisor Stephen Hadley, CPC General Secretary and PRC President Hu Jintao talked with President Bush on the phone, and Hu agreed to restore cross-strait "consultation" on the basis of the "1992 Consensus," explicitly entailing both sides recognizing one China but agree to differ on its definitions. *Xinhua*'s report in English also used this detailed phrase, but *Xinhua*'s report in Chinese referred only to the "1992 Consensus." In an interview reported in Chinese by *United Daily News* in Taipei on December 23, 2010, KMT President Ma Ying-jeou said that the CPC "recognized" the "1992 Consensus" and challenged the DPP to do so. Ma repeatedly used "1992 Consensus" rather than "One China, Different Interpretations." Ma went further to say that the DPP was the only one of four parties (which he called the ROC, mainland, the United States, and the DPP) not to accept the "1992 Consensus." However, the CPC's Taiwan Affairs Office (TAO) said on December 29 that both sides reached the "1992 Consensus," and the TAO did not refer to "one China, different interpretations." Moreover, the TAO still welcomed DPP members to visit the PRC. Also, contrary to Ma's characterization of U.S. policy as recognizing the "1992 Consensus," the State Department told Taiwan's *Liberty Times* on December 28 that: "Questions relating to establishing the basis for dialogue between Taiwan and the People's Republic of China are matters for the two parties to resolve. The U.S. takes no position on the substance of such questions. Our interest is that any resolution of cross-strait issues be peaceful."

[121] Press release in Chinese by the SEF, Taipei, November 3, 1992, printed in a book by a KMT politician: Su Chi, *The Historical Record of the Consensus of "One China, Different Interpretations"* (Taipei: National Policy Foundation, 2002). Also in "Strait Group Agrees to State Positions 'Orally'," *Central News Agency*, Taipei, November 18, 1992.

[122] *Renmin Ribao [People's Daily]*, Beijing, November 6, 1992. ARATS sent a letter to the SEF on November 16, 1992, reiterating this agreement. The letter also stated that "both sides of the strait support the one China principle and seek national unification. However, negotiations on routine matters across the strait do not involve the political meaning of 'one China'." The letter in Chinese is printed in a book by a KMT politician: Su Chi, *The Historical Record of the Consensus of "One China, Different Interpretations"* (Taipei: National Policy Foundation, a KMT think tank, 2002). Also reported in *Renmin Ribao*, November 21, 1992.

Statements During Clinton Administration

PRC Premier Li Peng Warns Taiwan[123]

March 15, 1993[124]

We advocate that both sides hold talks as soon as possible on bringing hostility between the two sides of the Taiwan Strait to an end and gradually fulfilling peaceful unification.... The forces advocating Taiwan independence on and off the island have resurged in recent years. Certain international forces have also deliberately created obstacles to impede China's peaceful unification. They cannot but arouse serious concern by the Chinese Government and all the Chinese people. We are resolutely opposed to any form of two China's or one China and one Taiwan; and we will take all necessary drastic measures to stop any activities aimed at making Taiwan independent and splitting the motherland.

Mainland-Taiwan "Koo-Wang" Talks (Singapore)[125]

April 27-29, 1993

PRC (Wang Daohan): *There are many questions that need to be solved because contacts between the two sides of the strait began only after a separation of more than 40 years. We have said repeatedly that as long as both sides sit down to talk, we can discuss any question. Proper methods for solving problems will be found as long as the two organizations observe the spirit of mutual respect, consult on equal footing, seek truth from facts, and seek common ground while reserving differences.*[126]

Taiwan (Koo Chen-fu): *There exist not only the same geographical, historical, and cultural origins between the two sides, but also a "blood is thicker than water" sentiment shared by our people. President Lee Teng-hui's proclamation that: "Taiwan's relationship with the entire Chinese people cannot be severed" could not have said it more clearly.*[127]

---

[123] PRC Premier Li Peng, Government Work Report to the First Session of the 8th National People's Congress, Beijing, *Central Television Program*, March 15, 1993; translated in *FBIS*, March 15, 1993. According to analysis by *FBIS Trends* (March 31, 1993), by saying "both sides" (not the Communist Party and the Nationalist Party), Li changed the formulation in his report from previous years, signaling greater PRC concern about pro-independence activities in Taiwan and urgency to hold unification talks, "as soon as possible." The analysis also noted that, when warning of "all necessary drastic measures," Li echoed the "unusually harsh language" used by General Secretary Jiang Zemin in December 1992. According to *Beijing Review* (January 4-10, 1993), Jiang warned that Beijing would take "resolute measures" to prevent Taiwan independence, while reiterating a policy of peaceful unification.

[124] PRC concern apparently increased after the first fully democratic legislative election was held in Taiwan on December 19, 1992. The ruling Nationalist Party (KMT) won 96 out of 161 seats, while the Democratic Progressive Party (DPP) gained 50 seats. The DPP has advocated a "Republic of Taiwan," instead of "Republic of China."

[125] Mainland Chinese and Taiwan authorities held their first talks and signed their first agreements since 1949. Represented by "authorized nongovernmental organizations," the PRC's Association for Relations Across the Taiwan Strait (ARATS) and Taiwan's Straits Exchange Foundation (SEF) met in Singapore and agreed to institutionalize contacts. ARATS Chairman Wang Daohan and SEF Chairman Koo Chen-fu agreed that the talks were not political, but were nongovernmental, economic, practical, and functional.

[126] *Xinhua (New China News Agency)*, Beijing, April 27, 1993, translated in FBIS, April 27, 1993.

[127] Dr. Koo's Arrival Address at Singapore Airport, April 26, 1993, "A Resume of the Koo-Wang Talks," Straits Exchange Foundation, December 1993.

Taiwan: *The subjects discussed in the Koo-Wang Talks were planned by the government in accord with the goals of the short-term phase in the Guidelines for National Unification.... The Koo-Wang Talks were obviously in no way political.... During the talks, SEF delegates steadfastly upheld the principle of parity in such matters as meeting procedures, conference site, seating, as well as the topics and scope of discussion. This made it impossible for the other side to slight the fact that the ROC is an equal political entity.*[128]

ROC (Taiwan)'s Bid to Gain Parallel Representation at the U.N.[129]

August-September 1993[130]

[In 1991], we accepted the fact that the nation was divided and that, prior to the unification of China, the political authority of both the ROC government and the Chinese communists exist. Both the ROC government and the Chinese communists exercise political authority in the areas under their de facto control. Each is entitled to represent the residents of the territory under its de facto control and to participate in the activities of the international community.... It is now the fixed policy and goal of the government and the opposition parties in the ROC to participate in the United Nations....

PRC's White Paper on Taiwan and on Military Option[131]

August 31, 1993

There is only one China in the world, Taiwan is an inalienable part of China, and the seat of China's central government is in Beijing. This is a universally recognized fact as well as the premise for a peaceful settlement of the Taiwan question. The Chinese government is firmly against any words or deeds designed to split China's sovereignty and territorial integrity. It opposes "two Chinas," "one China, one Taiwan," "one country, two governments," or any attempt or act that could lead to "independence of Taiwan." The Chinese people on both sides of the strait all believe that there is only one China and espouse national unification. Taiwan's status

---

[128] Mainland Affairs Council, ROC, "Our Views on the Koo-Wang Talks," May 1993.

[129] Jason Hu, Director of the ROC's Government Information Office, "The Case For Taipei's U.N. Representation," speech at the Atlantic Council on September 17, 1993. Hu said that Taiwan's bid was submitted in a letter sent by seven South American countries to the U.N. Secretary General on August 6, 1993. He said that the bid was flexible on the name to use at the U.N. See also: Fredrick F. Chien (ROC Foreign Minister), "UN Should Welcome Taiwan," *Far Eastern Economic Review,* August 5, 1993; "Divided China in the United Nations: Time for Parallel Representation" (advertisement), *New York Times,* September 17, 1993; and "Republic of China on Taiwan Observes 82nd Anniversary: New Goals Include Participation in the United Nations" (advertisement), *Washington Post,* October 7, 1993.

[130] On April 27-29, 1993, the landmark "Koo-Wang" talks had been held in Singapore between Koo Chen-fu (chairman of Taiwan's Strait Exchange Foundation (SEF)) and Wang Daohan (chairman of the PRC's Association for Relations Across the Taiwan Strait (ARATS)), the first meeting between the heads of the two organs set up for cross-strait dialogue. Later in 1993, according to Mann (p. 290), the State Department drafted a policy review to restore high-level dialogue with Beijing and submitted it to the White House in July 1993. As part of the new policy of engagement toward China, President Clinton invited PRC President Jiang Zemin to attend the first summit of leaders in the Asia Pacific Economic (APEC) Forum in Seattle, Washington, in November 1993. The *Far Eastern Economic Review* (October 7, 1993) reported that Taipei was concerned that Washington agreed with Beijing that Taiwan, despite its status in APEC equal to other members, would not be represented by Lee Teng-hui, but by Vincent Siew, head of economic planning.

[131] "The Taiwan Question and the Unification of China," *Xinhua [New China News Agency],* August 31, 1993, translated in *FBIS,* September 1, 1993.

as an inalienable part of China has been determined and cannot be changed. "Self-determination" for Taiwan is out of the question.

Peaceful unification is a set policy of the Chinese Government. However, any sovereign state is entitled to use any means it deems necessary, including military ones, to uphold its sovereignty and territorial integrity. The Chinese Government is under no obligation to undertake any commitment to any foreign power or people intending to split China as to what means it might use to handle its own domestic affairs.

It should be pointed out that the Taiwan question is purely an internal affair of China and bears no analogy to the cases of Germany and Korea which were brought about as a result of international accords at the end of the Second World War.

Taiwan's White Paper on Cross-Strait Relations[132]

July 5, 1994

It is an incontrovertible historical fact that the ROC has always been an independent sovereign state in the international community since its founding in 1912. However, relations between the two sides of the Taiwan Strait are not those between two separate countries, neither are they purely domestic in nature. In order to ensure that cross-strait relations develop toward benign interaction, the ROC government has formulated the concept of a "political entity" to serve as the basis of interaction between the two sides. The term "political entity" has extensive meaning, it can refer to a country, a government, or a political organization. At the current stage of cross-Strait interaction, only when we set aside the "sovereignty dispute" will we untie the knots that have bound us for more than the past 40 years and progress smoothly toward unification....

The ROC Government is firm in its advocacy of "one China" and is opposed to "two Chinas" or "one China, one Taiwan." But at the same time, given that division and divided rule on the two sides of the Taiwan Strait is a long-standing political fact, the ROC Government also holds that the two sides should be fully aware that each has jurisdiction over its respective territory and that they should coexist as two legal entities in the international arena. As for their relationship with each other, it is that of two separate areas of one China and is therefore "domestic" or "Chinese" in nature....

The ROC Government takes "one China, two equal political entities" as the structure for handling cross-strait relations and hopes that cross-strait relations will develop in the direction of being peaceful, pragmatic, and sensible. .. The CPC [Communist Party of China] should dismiss any misgivings it has concerning the ROC Government's determination to achieve unification. What the CPC authorities should give urgent consideration to is how, given the fact that the country is divided under two separate governments, we can actively create favorable conditions for unification and gradually bring the two different "political entities" together to form "one China." ... At the same time, the Chinese people cannot strive for unification just for the sake of unification; instead, unification should be realized under a reasonable and benign political, economic, and social system and way of living. Therefore, we hold that the two sides of the strait should go all out to build a democratic, free, equally wealthy, and united China....

---

[132] Mainland Affairs Council, Executive Yuan (Cabinet), Republic of China, "Explanation of Relations Across the Taiwan Strait," July 5, 1994, translated in *FBIS*, July 11, 1994.

Washington's 1994 Taiwan Policy Review[133]

September 7, 1994[134]

U.S. policy toward Taiwan is governed, of course, by the Taiwan Relations Act of 1979. Three communiques with the People's Republic of China (the Shanghai Communique of 1972, the Normalization Communique of 1979, and the Joint Communique of 1982) also constitute part of the foundation. In the joint communique shifting diplomatic relations to the PRC 15 years ago, the United States recognized "the Government of the People's Republic of China as the sole legal Government of China." The document further states that "Within this context, the people of the United States will maintain cultural, commercial, and other unofficial relations with the people of Taiwan." The United States also acknowledged "the Chinese position that there is but one China and Taiwan is part of China." These formulations were repeated in the 1982 communique. Since 1978, each Administration has reaffirmed this policy.

The policy has been essential in maintaining peace, stability, and economic development on both sides of the Taiwan Strait and throughout the region.... We have made absolutely clear our expectation that cross-strait relations will evolve in a peaceful manner. We neither interfere in nor mediate this process. But we welcome any evolution in relations between Taipei and Beijing that is mutually agreed upon and peacefully reached....

---

[133] Announced on September 7, 1994 and described in the Clinton Administration's only public statement on the Taiwan Policy Review, which was given by Assistant Secretary of State for East Asian and Pacific Affairs Winston Lord, "Taiwan Policy Review," Testimony before the Senate Foreign Relations Committee, September 27, 1994 (in *U.S. Department of State Dispatch*, October 17, 1994). Lord noted that "the lengthy, detailed inter-agency policy review that we have conducted is the first of its kind launched by any Administration of either political party since we shifted recognition to Beijing in 1979." While opposing legislation to specifically allow visits by top leaders of Taiwan, the Administration decided to send high-level economic and technical officials to visit Taiwan, establish a sub-cabinet level economic dialogue with Taiwan, allow Taiwan's office in the United States to change its name to Taipei Economic and Cultural Representative Office (TECRO), and support Taiwan's membership in international organizations where statehood is not a requirement and Taiwan's voice to be heard in organizations where its membership is not allowed.

[134] The review came after the Congress passed and the President signed (on April 30, 1994) the Foreign Relations Authorization Act for FY1994 and FY1995 (P.L. 103-236) which directed the State Department to register foreign-born Taiwanese-Americans as U.S. citizens born in Taiwan (rather than China); called for the President to send Cabinet-level officials to Taiwan and to show clear U.S. support for Taiwan in bilateral and multilateral relationships; and declared that Sec. 3 of the TRA (on arms sales) takes primacy over statements of U.S. policy (the 1982 communique). In addition, in May 1994, the State Department had allowed Taiwan President Lee Teng-hui to make a refueling stop in Hawaii but denied him a visa to enter the United States. In response, the Senate, from July to October, passed amendments introduced by Senator Brown to ensure that Taiwan's President can enter the United States on certain occasions. Two amendments (for S. 2182 and H.R. 4606) that passed were not retained, but the amendment to the Immigration and Nationality Technical Corrections Act of 1994 was enacted. Upon signing the bill into law (P.L. 103-416) on October 25, 1994, President Clinton, nonetheless, said that he would construe Sec. 221 as expressing Congress' view.

In the end, it is only the two parties themselves, Taiwan and the PRC, that will be able to resolve the issues between them. In this regard, the United States applauds the continuing progress in cross-strait dialogue....

We will continue to provide material and training to Taiwan to enable it to maintain a sufficient self-defense capability, as mandated by the Taiwan Relations Act....

Within this framework, the President has decided to enhance our unofficial ties with Taiwan.... the Administration strongly opposes Congressional attempts to legislate visits by top leaders of the "Republic of China" to the U.S....

Recognizing Taiwan's important role in transnational issues, we will support its membership in organizations where statehood is not a prerequisite, and will support opportunities for Taiwan's voice to be heard in organizations where its membership is not possible.

We do not seek and cannot impose a resolution of differences between Taiwan and the People's Republic of China. Nor should we permit one to manipulate us against the other.

PRC President Jiang Zemin's "Eight Points"[135]

January 30, 1995

1. We must firmly oppose any words or actions aimed at creating an "independent Taiwan" and the propositions "split the country and rule under separate regimes," two Chinas over a certain period of time," etc., which are in contravention of the principle of one China.

2. We do not challenge the development of non-governmental economic and cultural ties by Taiwan with other countries.... However, we oppose Taiwan's activities in "expanding its living space internationally," which are aimed at creating "two Chinas" or "one China, one Taiwan." ...

3. It has been our consistent stand to hold negotiations with the Taiwan authorities on the peaceful unification of the motherland.... I suggest that, as the first step, negotiations should be held and an agreement reached on officially ending the state of hostility between the two sides in accordance with the principle that there is only one China....

4. We should strive for the peaceful unification of the motherland, since Chinese should not fight fellow Chinese. Our not undertaking to give up the use of force is not directed against our compatriots in Taiwan but against the schemes of foreign forces to interfere with China's unification and to bring about the "independence of Taiwan." ...

5. Great efforts should be made to expand the economic exchanges and cooperation between the two sides of the Taiwan Strait...

---

[135] Jiang Zemin, "Continue to Promote the Unification of the Motherland," January 30, 1995. As part of the context of his speech, Jiang looked to the 100th anniversary of the Treaty of Shimonoseki, signed between China and Japan on April 17, 1895, which ceded Taiwan to Japan as a colony until the end of World War Two. Jiang also cited the transfer of control to the PRC of Hong Kong in 1997 and Macau in 1999, and said that "now it is high time to accomplish the unification of the motherland."

6. People on both sides of the Taiwan Strait should inherit and carry forward the fine traditions of Chinese culture.

7. The 21 million compatriots in Taiwan, whether born there or in other provinces, are all Chinese... We also hope that all political parties in Taiwan will adopt a sensible, forward-looking, and constructive attitude and promote the expansion of relations between the two sides....

8. Leaders of Taiwan authorities are welcome to pay visits in appropriate capacities. We are also ready to accept invitations from the Taiwan side to visit Taiwan.... The affairs of the Chinese people should be handled by ourselves, something that does not take an international occasion to accomplish....

Taiwan President Lee Teng-hui's "Six Point" Response[136]

April 8, 1995

1. The fact that the Chinese mainland and Taiwan have been ruled by two political entities in no way subordinate to each other had led to a state of division between the two sides and separate governmental jurisdictions, hence, the issue of national unification.... Only by facing up to this reality can both sides build greater consensus on the "one China" issue and at the earliest possible date.

2. In Taiwan, we have long taken upon ourselves the responsibility for safeguarding and furthering traditional Chinese culture, and advocate that culture be the basis for exchanges between both sides to help promote the nationalistic sentiment for living together in prosperity and to foster a strong sense of brotherliness....

3. We will continue to assist the mainland in developing its economy and upgrading the living standards of its people based upon our existing investments and trade relations. As for trade and transportation links with the mainland, the agencies concerned have to make in-depth evaluations as well as careful plans since these are very complicated issues....

4. I have indicated on several occasions that if leaders on both sides could meet with each other on international occasions in a natural manner, this would alleviate the political confrontation between both sides and foster a harmonious atmosphere for developing future relations.... It is our firm belief that the more international organizations both sides join on an equal footing, the more favorable the environment will become for the growth of bilateral relations and for the process of peaceful unification....

5. We believe the mainland authorities should demonstrate their goodwill by publicly renouncing the use of force and refrain from making any military move that might arouse anxiety or suspicion on this side of the Taiwan Strait, thus paving the way for formal negotiations between both sides to put an end to the state of hostility....

6. Hong Kong and Macau are integral parts of the Chinese nation ... Post-1997 Hong Kong and post-1999 Macau are naturally a matter of great concern to us. In this regard, the ROC

---

[136] Lee Teng-hui, "Address to the National Unification Council," April 8, 1995.

government has reiterated its determination to maintain normal contact with Hong Kong and Macau, further participate in affairs related to Hong Kong and Macau, and provide better services to our compatriots there....

U.S. Visa For Lee Teng-hui's Private Visit to Cornell University[137]

May 22, 1995

President Clinton has decided to permit Lee Teng-hui to make a private visit to the United States in June for the express purpose of participating in an alumni reunion event at Cornell University, as a distinguished alumnus. The action follows a revision of Administration guidelines to permit occasional private visits by senior leaders of Taiwan, including President Lee.

President Lee will visit the U.S. in a strictly private capacity and will not undertake any official activities. It is important to reiterate that this is not an official visit. The granting of a visa in this case is consistent with U.S. policy of maintaining only unofficial relations with Taiwan. It does not convey any change in our relations with or policies towards the People's Republic of China, with which we maintain official relations and recognize as the sole legal government of China.

We will continue to abide by the three communiques that form the basis of our relations with China. The United States also acknowledges the Chinese position that there is but one China, and Taiwan is a part of China....

Clinton's Secret Letter to Jiang Zemin and "Three Noes"[138]

August 1995

At a meeting in Brunei in August 1995, Secretary of State Warren Christopher reportedly delivered a letter from President Clinton to Chinese President Jiang Zemin. In the letter, which has not been made public, Clinton is said to have assured Jiang that the United States would (1) "oppose" Taiwan independence; (2) would not support "two Chinas," or one China and one Taiwan; and (3) would not support Taiwan's admission to the United Nations.

---

[137] Department of State's announcement by spokesperson, Nicholas Burns, May 22, 1995. Congress' view was an important factor acknowledged by the Administration in its reversal of policy to grant the visa. Congress had overwhelmingly passed the bipartisan H.Con.Res. 53 expressing the sense of Congress that the President should promptly welcome a visit by Lee Teng-hui to his alma mater, Cornell University, and a transit stop in Anchorage, Alaska, to attend a conference. The House passed the resolution by 396-0 on May 2, and the Senate passed it by 97-1 on May 9, 1995. Some analysts believe that another factor was the contrast posed by the Administration's March 1995 decision to grant visits to Gerry Adams (leader of Sinn Fein, the political wing of the Irish Republican Army (IRA)), to the United States, including meetings with Clinton in the White House—despite objections from London.

[138] Garver, p. 79; Mann, p. 330. These promises apparently formed the basis for the Administration's later public statements issued in 1997 and 1998, including one by President Clinton in China, that became known as the "Three Noes." However, "opposing" Taiwan independence was changed to a more neutral stance of "not supporting" it. Clinton's letter was sent after the People's Liberation Army (PLA) launched its first test-firing of M-9 short-range ballistic missiles toward Taiwan in July 1995, as part of the PRC's reaction to Lee Teng-hui's visit to Cornell University in June 1995.

U.S. State Department and 1995-1996 Taiwan Strait Crisis[139]

March 14, 1996

Our fundamental interest on the Taiwan question is that peace and stability be maintained and that the PRC and Taiwan work out their differences peacefully. At the same time, we will strictly avoid interfering as the two sides pursue peaceful resolution of differences.

The Taiwan Relations Act (TRA) of 1979 forms the legal basis of U.S. policy regarding the security of Taiwan.... However serious, the present situation does not constitute a threat to Taiwan of the magnitude contemplated by the drafters of the Taiwan Relations Act. The PRC pressure against Taiwan to date does not add up to a "threat to the security or the social or economic system" of Taiwan....We will continue to work closely with you, and if warranted by circumstances, we will act under Section 3(c) of the TRA, in close consultation with the Congress.

Overall U.S. China policy, including the Taiwan question, is expressed in the three joint communiques with the PRC as follows:

—The United States recognizes the Government of the PRC as "the sole legal Government of China."

—The U.S. acknowledges the Chinese position that "there is but one China and Taiwan is part of China." In 1982, the U.S. assured the PRC that it has no intention of pursuing a policy of "two Chinas" or "one China, one Taiwan."

—Within this context, the people of the U.S. will maintain cultural, commercial, and other unofficial relations with the people of Taiwan.

—The U.S. has consistently held that resolution of the Taiwan issue is a matter to be worked out peacefully by the Chinese themselves.

President Clinton's Meeting with Japanese Prime Minister[140]

April 17, 1996

Clinton: *Yes, we discussed Taiwan and China extensively, as well as the recent tension in the strait. It is obvious that our partnership is designed to try to preserve the peace for all peoples in*

---

[139] Department of State, Winston Lord, Assistant Secretary of State for East Asian and Pacific Affairs, Testimony before the House International Relations Subcommittee on East Asia and the Pacific, March 14, 1996. The PRC followed its July 1995 missile test-firings with more military exercises and additional missile test-firings in March 1996—to intimidate voters in Taiwan on the eve of their first democratic presidential election. After introduction of H.Con.Res. 148 on March 7, 1996, the Clinton Administration announced on March 10 and 11 the decisions to deploy two carrier battle groups east of Taiwan to underscore the American commitment to regional peace and stability. However, the Administration did not agree with Congress on the need to formally consult with Congress on the U.S. response to the PLA actions, under Section 3(c) of the TRA.

[140] "The President's News Conference with Prime Minister Ryutaro Hashimoto of Japan in Tokyo," April 17, 1996, *Public Papers of United States Presidents, William Clinton.* The two leaders issued a Joint Declaration on Security to strengthen the alliance.

---

this region. And I believe that I can say we both agree that, while the United States clearly observes the so-called one China policy, we also observe the other aspects of the agreement we made many years ago, which include a commitment on the part of both parties to resolve all their differences in a peaceable manner. And we have encouraged them to pursue that. Therefore, we were concerned about those actions in the Taiwan Strait.

Secretary of State Christopher on Relations with China[141]

May 17, 1996

Since 1972, the foundation for deepening engagement between our nations has been the "one China" policy that is embodied in the three joint communiques between the United States and the People's Republic of China....

The United States strongly believes that resolution of the issues between the PRC and Taiwan must be peaceful. We were gravely concerned when China's military exercises two months ago raised tensions in the Taiwan Strait. Our deployment of naval forces to the region was meant to avert any dangerous miscalculations. We are encouraged that both sides have now taken steps to reduce tensions.

On the eve of the inauguration next Monday of Taiwan's first democratically elected President, it is timely to reflect on the enduring value of our "one China" policy for both the PRC and Taiwan and on our common interest and responsibility to uphold it. I want to tell you publicly today what we have been saying privately to the leaders in Beijing and Taipei in recent weeks.

To the leadership in Beijing, we have reiterated our consistent position that the future relationship between Taiwan and the PRC must be resolved directly between them. But we have reaffirmed that we have a strong interest in the region's continued peace and stability and that our "one China" policy is predicated on the PRC's pursuit of a peaceful resolution of issues between Taipei and Beijing.

To the leadership in Taiwan, we have reiterated our commitment to robust unofficial relations, including helping Taiwan maintain a sufficient self-defense capacity under the terms of the Taiwan Relations Act. We have stressed that Taiwan has prospered under the "one China" policy. And we have made clear our view that as Taiwan seeks an international role, it should pursue that objective in a way that is consistent with a "one China" policy.

We have emphasized to both sides the importance of avoiding provocative actions or unilateral measures that would alter the status quo or pose a threat to peaceful resolution of outstanding

---

[141] Department of State, "American Interests and the U.S.-China Relationship," Address by Secretary of State Warren Christopher to the Asia Society, the Council on Foreign Relations, and the National Committee on U.S.-China Relations, New York, May 17, 1996. Christopher ended with a signal of President Clinton's new willingness to hold regular summits with the PRC President. Then in July 1996, National Security Advisor Anthony Lake traveled to China to pursue the "strategic dialogue." Briefing reporters on July 3, 1996, a National Security Council official said Lake was scheduled to meet Wang Daohan, chairman of the Association for Relations Across the Taiwan Strait (ARATS), in order to do "what we can there to advance the resumption and to promote the resumption of cross-strait dialogue and to reinforce our position that the differences between Taiwan and China need to be resolved peacefully." This item on Lake's agenda signaled a new, proactive U.S. stance on cross-strait relations and raised questions in Beijing and Taipei of U.S. involvement. The meeting was canceled after Lake's arrival in China.

issues. And we have strongly urged both sides to resume the cross-strait dialogue that was interrupted last summer.

Taiwan's First Direct Presidential Election and Inaugural Address[142]

May 20, 1996

The Republic of China has always been a sovereign state. Disputes across the Strait center around system and lifestyle; they have nothing to do with ethnic or cultural identity. Here in this country, it is totally unnecessary or impossible to adopt the so-called course of "Taiwan independence." For over 40 years, the two sides of the Strait have been two separate jurisdictions due to various historical factors, but it is also true that both sides pursue eventual national unification....

Taiwan's Multi-Party National Development Conference[143]

December 23-28, 1996

The Republic of China has been a sovereign state since 1912. Following the establishment of the Chinese communist regime in 1949, both sides of the Taiwan Strait became co-equal political entities....

The development of relations with the mainland must be based on safeguarding the survival and development of the Republic of China....

The Republic of China is a sovereign state that must actively promote foreign relations and raise its profile at international activities in its pursuit of national survival and development. Taiwan is not a part of the "People's Republic of China," and the ROC government opposes dealing with the cross-strait issue through the "one country, two systems" scheme.

The government should reduce the possibility of confrontation with the mainland by establishing sound mainland policies, and should actively make use of regional and global security and cooperation mechanisms to assure the security of Taiwan.

At this point, ROC accession to such international bodies as the World Trade Organization, the International Monetary Fund, and the World Bank, should continue to be actively pursued.

---

[142] "The President [Lee Teng-hui's] Inaugural Speech (Excerpt),"May 20, 1996, printed in *Consensus Formed at the National Development Conference on Cross-Strait Relations,* Mainland Affairs Council, Executive Yuan, Republic of China, February 1997. With a tense military environment brought by China's military exercises that included missile test-firings, Lee Teng-hui won a landslide victory of 54 percent of the votes in Taiwan's first democratic presidential election on March 23, 1996. Pro-independence candidate Peng Ming-min received 21 percent, and pro-unification Lin Yang-kang won 15 percent of the votes.

[143] *Consensus Formed at the National Development Conference on Cross-Strait Relations,* Mainland Affairs Council, Executive Yuan, Republic of China, February 1997. Also see CRS Report 97-268, *Taiwan's National Development Conference: Proposed Policy Changes and Implications for the United States,* by Robert G. Sutter. Called by President Lee Teng-hui in his inaugural speech in May 1996, delegates from the three major political parties (Nationalist Party, Democratic Progressive Party, and New China Party) attended the conference. The conference took place as Taiwan looked to the transfer of Hong Kong as a British colony to a Special Administration Region of the PRC in July 1997.

ROC admission to the United Nations should be actively pursued as a long-term objective through flexible responses to changes in the international situation.

President Clinton's Statements at the 1997 Summit

October 29, 1997

A key to Asia's stability is a peaceful and prosperous relationship between the People's Republic of China and Taiwan. I reiterated America's longstanding commitment to a one China policy. It has allowed democracy to flourish in Taiwan and provides a framework in which all three relationships can prosper—between the United States and the PRC, the United States and Taiwan, and Taiwan and the People's Republic of China. I told President Jiang that we hope the People's Republic and Taiwan would resume a constructive cross-strait dialogue and expand cross-strait exchanges. Ultimately, the relationship between the PRC and Taiwan is for the Chinese themselves to determine—peacefully.[144]

First of all, I think the most important thing the United States can do to facilitate a peaceful resolution of the differences is to adhere strictly to the one China policy we have agreed on, to make it clear that within the context of that one China policy, as articulated in the communiques and our own laws, we will maintain friendly, open relations with the people of Taiwan and China; but that we understand that this issue has to be resolved and resolved peacefully, and that if it is resolved in a satisfactory way, consistent with statements made in the past, then Asia will be stronger and more stable and more prosperous. That is good for the United States. And our own relations with China will move on to another stage of success. I think the more we can encourage that, the better off we are. But I think in the end, since so much investment and contact has gone on in the last few years between Taiwan and China, I think the Chinese people know how to resolve this when the time is right, and we just have to keep saying we hope the time will be right as soon as possible. Sooner is better than later.[145]

1997 Clinton-Jiang Summit and U.S.-China Joint Statement[146]

October 29, 1997

China stresses that the Taiwan question is the most important and sensitive central question in China-U.S. relations, and that the proper handling of this question in strict compliance with the principles set forth in the three China-U.S. joint communiques holds the key to sound and stable growth of China-U.S. relations. The United States reiterates that it adheres to its "one China" policy and the principles set forth in the three U.S.-China joint communiques.

---

[144] President Clinton's opening statement, Press Conference by President Clinton and President Jiang Zemin, Old Executive Office Building, Washington, DC, October 29, 1997.

[145] President Clinton's answer to a question about whether he sees any U.S. role in securing a permanent peaceful environment in the Taiwan Strait (after reference to U.S. roles in brokering peace in Bosnia and the Middle East), Press Conference by President Clinton and President Jiang Zemin, Old Executive Office Building, Washington, DC, October 29, 1997.

[146] White House, "Joint U.S.-China Statement," October 29, 1997. In preparing for the summit, the PRC desired to have a "fourth communique" with further U.S. assurances on Taiwan. Also, Mann wrote that the PRC wanted the joint statement to make public the "Three Noes" that President Clinton had promised President Jiang in a private letter in 1995. The Joint Statement did not mention the TRA.

1997 Summit and the State Department on the "Three Noes"[147]

October 31, 1997

We certainly made clear that we have a one-China policy; that we don't support a one-China, one-Taiwan policy. We don't support a two-China policy. We don't support Taiwan independence, and we don't support Taiwanese membership in organizations that require you to be a member state. We certainly made that very clear to the Chinese.

1998 Clinton-Jiang Summit in Beijing[148]

June 27, 1998

President Jiang: *The Taiwan question is the most important and the most sensitive issue at the core of China-U.S. relations. We hope that the U.S. side will adhere to the principles set forth in the three China-U.S. joint communiques and the joint China-U.S. statement, as well as the relevant commitments it has made in the interest of a smooth growth of China-U.S. relations.*

President Clinton: *I reaffirmed our longstanding one China policy to President Jiang and urged the pursuit of cross-strait discussions recently resumed as the best path to a peaceful resolution. In a similar vein, I urged President Jiang to assume a dialogue with the Dalai Lama in return for the recognition that Tibet is a part of China and in recognition of the unique cultural and religious heritage of that region.*

---

[147] Department of State, Press Briefing by James Rubin, October 31, 1997. For the first time, the Administration publicly stated the "Three Noes," which were not put in writing in the U.S.-China Joint Statement. Rubin made that statement in response to a question about specific assurances on Taiwan that President Clinton gave to President Jiang during the 1997 summit. Clinton reportedly had passed a secret letter to Jiang in August 1995 with an earlier version of the "Three Noes."

[148] White House, Office of the Press Secretary, "Press Availability by President Clinton and President Jiang," Beijing, PRC, June 27, 1998.

1998 Summit and Clinton's Statement on the "Three Noes"[149]

June 30, 1998[150]

I had a chance to reiterate our Taiwan policy, which is that we don't support independence for Taiwan, or two Chinas, or one Taiwan-one China. And we don't believe that Taiwan should be a member in any organization for which statehood is a requirement. So I think we have a consistent policy. Our only policy has been that we think it has to be done peacefully. That is what our law says, and we have encouraged the cross-strait dialogue. And I think eventually it will bear fruit if everyone is patient and works hard.

Taiwan's Lee Teng-hui on "One Divided China"[151]

August 3, 1998

The path to a democratic China must begin with a recognition of the present reality by both sides of the Taiwan Strait. And that reality is that China is divided, just as Germany and Vietnam were in the past and as Korea is today. Hence, there is no "one China" now. We hope for this outcome in the future, but presently it does not exist. Today, there is only "one divided China," with Taiwan and the mainland each being part of China. Because neither has jurisdiction over the other, neither can represent the other, much less all of China.

---

[149] White House, Office of the Press Secretary, "Remarks by the President and the First Lady in Discussion on Shaping China for the 21st Century," Shanghai, China, June 30, 1998. The Administration maintains that the "Three Noes" represented no change in U.S. policy. Nonetheless, President Clinton chose to issue this statement verbally and at an informal "roundtable discussion," rather than at the summit in Beijing with President Jiang on June 27, 1998. In testimony to the Senate Foreign Relations Committee on March 25, 1999, Assistant Secretary of State Stanley Roth cited Kissinger's 1971 promise as the origins of U.S. policy of non-support for Taiwan's independence and argued that President Clinton's June 1998 "Three Noes" statement represented no change in U.S. policy toward Taiwan.

[150] On the eve of President Clinton's trip to China, Deputy Assistant Secretary of State Susan Shirk testified before the House International Relations Subcommittee on Asia and the Pacific on May 20, 1998, stating that "there will be no fourth communique; nor will our relationship with Taiwan be diluted or sacrificed in any way." Deputy Assistant Secretary of Defense Kurt Campbell also assured Congress that "there will be no fourth communique and there will be no document that harms Taiwan's interest." The House, on June 9, 1998, passed (411-0) H.Con.Res. 270 (Solomon), resolving that it is the sense of Congress that "the United States abides by all previous understandings of a 'one China' policy and its abiding interest in a peaceful resolution of the Taiwan Strait issue." The House also resolved that the President should seek at the summit a public renunciation by the PRC of any use of force or threat to use force against Taiwan. After the President stated the "Three Noes" in China, the Senate passed (92-0) S.Con.Res. 107 (Lott) on July 10, 1998, affirming its expectation that the future of Taiwan will be determined by peaceful means, but did not include language on the people of both sides of the strait determining their own future. The House, on July 20, 1998, passed (390-1) H.Con.Res. 301 (DeLay) affirming its expectation that the "future status of Taiwan will be determined by peaceful means, and that the people of both sides of the Taiwan Strait should determine their own future ... " Also see CRS Report 98-837, *Taiwan: The "Three No's," Congressional-Administration Differences, and U.S. Policy Issues,* by Robert G. Sutter.

[151] Lee Teng-hui, "U.S. Can't Ignore Taiwan," *Wall Street Journal,* August 3, 1998.

Second "Koo-Wang Talks" (Shanghai)[152]

October 14, 1998

Taiwan: *It has been nearly 50 years since the two sides of the Taiwan Strait became two equal entities under divided rule and not subordinate to each other. A "divided China" is not only a historical fact, but also a political reality.*[153]

Taiwan: *China's unification hinges upon the democratization of the Chinese mainland. Only when the Chinese mainland has achieved democracy can the two sides of the Taiwan Strait talk about unification.*[154]

PRC: *Mr. Wang said that Taiwan's political status can be discussed under the one China principle. On this point, both Mr. Jiang Zemin and Mr. Qian Qichen had similar comments to the effect that anything can be put on the table under the one China principle. Therefore, on the question of one China, this will be our consistent stand before the two sides across the strait are reunified: there is only one China across the strait, Taiwan is part of China, and Chinese sovereignty and territorial integrity are indivisible.... Now, the Government of the People's Republic of China is universally acknowledged internationally as the only legitimate government representing China. In spite of this, the two sides should still negotiate on equal footing under the principle that there is but one China. The issue of whether the talks are between central or local authorities can be left aside.*[155]

U.S. Assistant Secretary Stan Roth on "Interim Agreements"[156]

March 24, 1999

Insisting on peaceful resolution of differences between the PRC and Taiwan will remain U.S. policy in the future just as surely as it has been our policy over the past twenty years. Our belief, which we have stated repeatedly, is that dialogue between the PRC and Taiwan fosters an atmosphere in which tensions are reduced, misperceptions can be clarified, and common ground can be explored. The exchange of visits under the SEF/ARATS framework, currently rich in

---

[152] ARATS and SEF agreed on a four-point common understanding: (hold all kinds of dialogue, including political and economic dialogue; strengthen exchanges, including those at all levels; strengthen mutual assistance in cases involving lives and property; acceptance of an invitation for Wang Daohan to visit Taiwan at an appropriate time), according to *Xinhua Hong Kong Service*, October 15, 1998, in *FBIS*.

[153] Koo Chen-fu, "Key Points From Remarks Made at a Meeting with ARATS Chairman Wang Daohan," Shanghai, October 14, 1998 (issued by SEF, Republic of China).

[154] Opening remarks of Taiwan's SEF Chairman Koo Chen-fu at a press conference after his meeting with PRC President Jiang Zemin in Beijing, October 18, 1998.

[155] Statement of Tang Shubei, executive vice chairman of the PRC's ARATS, denying inconsistency between comments of ARATS chairman Wang Daohan and Vice Premier Qian Qichen, "Tang Shubei Explains 'One China' Principle," *Zhongguo Xinwen She* (China News Agency), Beijing, October 18, 1998; translated in *FBIS*.

[156] Stanley O. Roth, Assistant Secretary of State for East Asian and Pacific Affairs, "The Taiwan Relations Act at Twenty—and Beyond," address to the Woodrow Wilson Center and the American Institute in Taiwan, Washington, DC, March 24, 1999. On the next day, Roth testified before the Senate Foreign Relations Committee on U.S.-Taiwan relations, but he did not discuss the possibility of cross-strait "interim agreements." He also assured the committee that "the future of cross-strait relations is a matter for Beijing and Taipei to resolve. No Administration has taken a position on how or when they should do so."

---

symbolism but still nascent in substance, has the potential to contribute to the peaceful resolution of difficult substantive differences.

Clearly, this will not be easy, but this Administration has great confidence in the creativity of the people of Taiwan and the people of the mainland, working together, to identify the necessary human contacts and the most comfortable processes to give the dialogue real meaning. Using a phrase that has garnered much favor in Washington of late, I could imagine that "out of the box" thinking within this dialogue might contribute to interim agreements, perhaps in combination with specific confidence building measures, on any number of difficult topics. But, as the U.S. has steadfastly held, we will avoid interfering as the two sides pursue peaceful resolution of differences, because it is only the participants on both sides of the strait that can craft the specific solutions which balance their interests while addressing their most pressing concerns.

Taiwan's Lee Teng-hui on "Special State-to-State" Relations[157]

July 9, 1999[158]

The fact that disregarding the reality that the two sides of the Taiwan Strait are under separate administrations of different governments, the Chinese communist authorities have been threatening us with force is actually the main reason why cross-strait ties cannot be improved thoroughly.... Since the PRC's establishment, the Chinese communists have never ruled Taiwan, Penghu, Kinmen, and Matsu, which have been under the jurisdiction of the Republic of China.... Since our constitutional reform in 1991, we have designated cross-strait ties as nation-to-nation, or at least as special state-to-state ties, rather than internal ties within "one China" between a legitimate government and a rebellion group, or between central and local governments....

President Clinton on the "Three Pillars" of Policy Toward Taiwan[159]

July 21, 1999

Clinton [on whether the United States is obligated to defend Taiwan militarily if it abandons the one China policy and would continue to provide military aid if Taiwan pursues separatism]: *Well, let me say first of all, a lot of those questions are governed by the Taiwan Relations Act, which we intend to honor. Our policy is clear: We favor the one China policy; we favor the cross-strait dialogues. The understanding we have had all along with both China and Taiwan is that the differences between them would be resolved peacefully. If that were not to be the case, under the Taiwan Relations Act we would be required to view it with the gravest concern....*

---

[157] President Lee Teng-hui's interview with the Voice of Germany, Taipei, July 9, 1999, reported in *Chung-Yang Jih-Pao*, July 10, 1999, in *FBIS*. Lee was responding to a question about Beijing viewing Taiwan as a "renegade province." Some observers note that Lee may have specifically chosen German media, because Germany was once a divided country.

[158] Three days later, Taiwan's Mainland Affairs Council Chairman Su Chi added that "While we continue to show our goodwill, Mainland China continues to tighten its 'one China principle.' Therefore, it is unnecessary for us to stick to our previous position. We shall clearly define equal footing in order to usher in better cross-strait relations toward the next century." From: "MAC Chairman Su Chi at July 12, 1999 Press Conference," *Taipei Speaks Up: Special State-to-State Relationship, Republic of China's Policy Documents*, Mainland Affairs Council, Executive Yuan, Republic of China, August 1999.

[159] White House, Office of the Press Secretary, "Press Conference by the President," Washington, DC, July 21, 1999.

Clinton [on delaying a Pentagon delegation's visit to Taiwan]: *I didn't think this was the best time to do something which might excite either one side or the other and imply that a military solution is an acceptable alternative. If you really think about what's at stake here, it would be unthinkable. And I want—I don't want to depart from any of the three pillars. I think we need to stay with one China; I think we need to stay with the dialogue; and I think that no one should contemplate force here.*

Taiwan's Position Paper on "Special State-to-State Relationship"[160]

August 1, 1999

President Lee's remarks concerning the nature of the cross-strait relationship were based on the necessity of protecting national interests and dignity. From the political, historical, and legal perspectives, he merely clarified an existing fact. He by no means twisted or exaggerated the truth, nor did he exclude the goal of unifying both sides of the Strait as a new, democratic China....

Taiwan and the Chinese mainland have always differed in their definition of "one China." Thus, in 1992, ... the two sides eventually reached an agreement on "one China, with each side being entitled to its respective interpretation." ... However, Beijing has unilaterally abandoned this agreement in recent years.... In the framework of the 1992 agreement, whereby each side is entitled to its respective interpretation, we have always maintained that the "one China" concept refers to the future rather than the present. The two sides are not yet unified, but are equals, ruled separately. We both exist concurrently. Therefore, the two sides can be defined as sharing a "special state-to-state relationship," prior to unification....

Presidents Clinton and Jiang at APEC Meeting[161]

September 11, 1999[162]

Clinton [on his message concerning Taiwan]: *My message is that our policy has not and will not change. We favor one China. We favor a peaceful approach to working out the differences. We favor the cross-strait dialogue. Our policy has not changed and it will not change.*

Jiang [on whether the PRC will maintain its threat to use military force against Taiwan]: *Our policy on Taiwan is a consistent one. That is, one, peaceful unification, one country-two systems.*

---

[160] "Parity, Peace, and Win-Win: The Republic of China's Position on the 'Special State-to-State Relationship'," Mainland Affairs Council, Executive Yuan, Republic of China, August 1, 1999.

[161] White House, Office of the Press Secretary, "Remarks by the President and President Jiang Zemin of the People's Republic of China in Photo Opportunity," Auckland, New Zealand, September 11, 1999. In a press briefing just after President Clinton's meeting with Jiang, National Security Advisor Sandy Berger said that Clinton told Jiang that if he were to resort to military force, "there would be grave consequences in the United States." Berger said Clinton also stated that U.S. policy would continue "as it has been since the presidency of Richard Nixon," to be based on the "three fundamental pillars" of the one China policy, a peaceful resolution of the Taiwan issue, and the cross-strait dialogue.

[162] A few days, later, on September 15, 1999, the United States spoke out, for the first time, against the ROC's bid for re-entering the United Nations, reported *Reuters*. Previously, the United States remained outside the debate on whether to place the issue of the ROC's membership on the General Assembly's agenda. This year, an unnamed U.S. official was quoted: "we wanted to make clear that our 'one-China' policy is unchanged." The annual outcome, since Taiwan's effort began in 1993, has been a failure to get the issue of its membership on the agenda.

However, if there were to be any foreign intervention, or if there were to be Taiwan independence, then we would not undertake to renounce the use of force.

PRC's Second Taiwan White Paper and "Three Ifs"[163]

February 21, 2000[164]

On October 1, 1949, the Central People's Government of the PRC was proclaimed, replacing the government of the Republic of China to become the only legal government of the whole of China and its sole legal representative in the international arena, thereby bringing the historical status of the Republic of China to an end.... so the government of the PRC naturally should fully enjoy and exercise China's sovereignty, including its sovereignty over Taiwan....

The Chinese government is actively and sincerely striving for peaceful unification. To achieve peaceful unification, the Chinese government has appealed time and again for cross-strait negotiations on the basis of equality and the One China principle.... The Chinese government has also proposed that dialogue (that includes political dialogue) may start first, which may gradually move on to procedural consultations for political negotiation (to resolve issues for formal negotiation, such as the name, topics for discussion, and format), then political negotiation may begin. Political negotiation may be carried out step-by-step....

However, since the early 1990s, Lee Teng-hui has gradually deviated from the One China principle... In military affairs, the Taiwan authorities have bought large quantities of advanced weapons from foreign countries and sought to join the TMD system, attempting to covertly establish certain forms of military alliance with the United States and Japan....

Facts prove that a serious crisis still exists in the situation of the Taiwan Strait. To safeguard the interests of the entire Chinese people, including compatriots in Taiwan, and maintain the peace and development of the Asia-Pacific region, the Chinese government remains firm in adhering to "peaceful unification, one country/two systems;" upholding the eight propositions put forward by President Jiang Zemin for the development of cross-strait relations and the acceleration of the peaceful unification of China; and doing its utmost to achieve the objective of peaceful

---

[163] The PRC's Taiwan Affairs Office and Information Office of the State Council, "The One China Principle and the Taiwan Issue," February 21, 2000, the English version as published by *Xinhua [New China News Agency]* and translated in *FBIS*, and the Chinese version as published by *People's Daily Online*.

[164] The PRC issued this white paper just after a U.S. delegation left Beijing. The delegation included Deputy National Security Advisor James Steinberg, Under Secretary of Defense Walter Slocombe, Vice Chairman of the Joint Chiefs of Staff General Joseph Ralston, and Deputy Secretary of State Strobe Talbott, who were given no indication that the white paper would be issued. The white paper was also issued on the eve of Taiwan's presidential election scheduled for March 18, 2000, with the possibility that Chen Shui-bian would win. Moreover, the House had passed (341-70) H.R. 1838, "the Taiwan Security Enhancement Act," on February 1, 2000, which was still pending in the Senate and opposed by Beijing and the Clinton Administration. News reports also said that Taipei and Washington were discussing Taiwan's possible procurement of Aegis-equipped destroyers, missile defense systems, and other advanced U.S. weapons, leading to annual arms sales talks in April. In his response to the PRC's White Paper on Taiwan, Undersecretary of Defense Walter Slocombe, who just returned from Beijing, warned on February 22 that the PRC would face "incalculable consequences" if it used force against Taiwan as the White Paper threatened (*Washington Post*, February 23, 2000). On the same day, Assistant Secretary of State Stanley Roth testified to the Senate Foreign Relations Subcommittee on East Asian and Pacific Affairs that "the threat of the use of force to resolve the Taiwan question is contrary to the commitments contained in the communiques that are the bedrock of U.S. policy." In his comments about the White Paper, Roth also reiterated the Administration's "three principles" (peaceful resolution, cross-strait dialogue, and one China).

---

unification. However, if a grave turn of events occurs leading to the separation of Taiwan from China in any name, or if there is foreign invasion and occupation of Taiwan,[165] or if Taiwan authorities indefinitely refuse to peacefully resolve the cross-strait unification problem through negotiations, then the Chinese government will only be forced to adopt all possible drastic measures, including the use of force, to safeguard China's sovereignty and territorial integrity, and fulfill the great cause of China's unification....

Countries maintaining diplomatic relations with China must not sell arms to Taiwan or enter into any forms of military alliance with Taiwan ... or help Taiwan to produce weapons....

President Clinton on Resolution with "Assent" of Taiwan's People[166]

February 24, 2000

We'll continue to reject the use of force as a means to resolve the Taiwan question. We'll also continue to make absolutely clear that the issues between Beijing and Taiwan must be resolved peacefully and with the assent of the people of Taiwan.

Taiwan President Chen's Inauguration Speech and "Five Noes"[167]

May 20, 2000[168]

Today, as the Cold War has ended, it is time for the two sides to cast aside the hostilities left from the old era. We do not need to wait further because now is a new opportunity for the two sides to create an era of reconciliation together.

The people across the Taiwan Strait share the same ancestral, cultural, and historical background. While upholding the principles of democracy and parity, building upon the existing foundations, and constructing conditions for cooperation through goodwill, we believe that the leaders on both sides possess enough wisdom and creativity to jointly deal with the question of a future "one China."

I fully understand that as the popularly elected 10th-term President of the Republic of China, I must abide by the Constitution, maintain the sovereignty, dignity, and security of our country, and ensure the well-being of all citizens. Therefore, as long as the CCP regime has no intention to use military force against Taiwan, I pledge that during my term in office, I will not declare independence, I will not change the national title, I will not push forth the inclusion of the so-

---

[165] This second phrase can be interpreted to mean U.S. involvement in Taiwan's defense.

[166] Remarks by the President to the Business Council, February 24, 2000. Later, Clinton added a third point, saying also that "there must be a shift from threat to dialogue across the Taiwan Strait, and we will continue to encourage both sides to seize this opportunity after the Taiwan election" (Remarks by the President on China, March 8, 2000).

[167] ROC, Office of the President, "Taiwan Stands Up: Toward the Dawn of a Rising Era," May 20, 2000 (English and Chinese versions via the Government Information Office).

[168] On March 18, 2000, Chen Shui-bian of the Democratic Progressive Party (DPP) won the presidential election in Taiwan with 39 percent of the vote. Independent candidate James Soong won 37 percent. The ruling Kuomintang (KMT), or Nationalist Party's, Lien Chan won 23 percent. The DPP has leaned toward favoring Taiwan's independence. Chen's DPP administration brought Taiwan's first democratic transfer of power from one party to another, after 55 years of KMT rule.

called "state-to-state" description in the Constitution, and I will not promote a referendum to change the status quo in regards to the question of independence or unification. Furthermore, the abolition of the National Unification Council or the Guidelines for National Unification will not be an issue.

PRC Vice Premier Qian Qichen's New Formulation[169]

July-August 2000[170]

With regard to cross-strait relations, the one China principle we stand for is that there is only one China in the world; the mainland and Taiwan all belong to one China; and China's sovereignty and territorial integrity are indivisible.

Taiwan President Chen on "Integration"[171]

December 31, 2000

I have always felt that the people on both sides of the Taiwan Strait came from the same family and that they all pursue the same goals of peaceful coexistence and mutual prosperity. Since both sides with to live under the same roof, we should be more understanding and helpful rather than harming or destroying each other.... The integration of our economies, trade, and culture can be a starting point for gradually building faith and confidence in each other. This, in turn, can be the basis for a new framework of permanent peace and political integration.

---

[169] *Xinhua* [New China News Agency], August 25, 2000, in FBIS.

[170] In July 2000, while meeting with visiting Taiwan lawmakers and journalists, Qian Qichen began to articulate this more flexible formulation of the "one China" principle, particularly in saying that the mainland and Taiwan both belong to one China (vs. that Taiwan is a part of the PRC or China), according to Taiwan media (e.g., *Central News Agency*, July 18, 2000). Later, looking towards an incoming Bush Administration, Qian granted an interview at Zhongnanhai (the leadership compound) to the *Washington Post* to reiterate what he described as a new flexibility on Taiwan to the United States (John Pomfret, "Beijing Signals New Flexibility on Taiwan," *Washington Post*, January 5, 2001). In a speech on January 11, 2001, outgoing Assistant Secretary of State Stanley Roth praised the "significant formulation by Vice Premier Qian Qichen to the effect that the PRC and Taiwan are both parts of China." In an interview with the *Washington Post* (March 24, 2001), however, President Jiang Zemin ruled out applying the models of confederation or federation.

[171] Chen Shui-bian, President of the Republic of China, "Bridging the New Century: New Year's Eve Address," December 31, 2000. For "integration," Chen used "*tong he.*"

Statements During George W. Bush Administration

President Bush on "Whatever It Takes"[172]

April 25, 2001

On ABC: *[If Taiwan were attacked by the PRC, the United States has an obligation to use] whatever it took to help Taiwan defend herself.*

On CNN: *Well, I think that the Chinese must hear that ours is an administration, like other administrations, that is willing to uphold the spirit of the ... Taiwan Relations Act. And I'll do so. However, I think it's important for people to also note that mine is an administration that strongly supports the one China policy, that we expect any dispute to be resolved peacefully. And that's the message I really want people to hear. But as people have seen, that I'm willing to help Taiwan defend herself, and that nothing has really changed in policy, as far as I'm concerned. This is what other presidents have said, and I will continue to say so.... I have said that I will do what it takes to help Taiwan defend herself, and the Chinese must understand that. Secondly, I certainly hope Taiwan adheres to the one China policy. And a declaration of independence is not the one China policy, and we will work with Taiwan to make sure that that doesn't happen. We need a peaceful resolution of this issue.*

PRC Vice Premier Qian Qichen's Invitation to the DPP[173]

January 24, 2002[174]

The refusal to accept the principle of one China and recognize the "1992 consensus" by the leader of the Taiwan authorities is the crucial reason leading to a deadlock in cross-strait relations and also the root cause of instability of the situation and possible danger in the Taiwan Strait.... We hold that political differences must not interfere with economic and trade exchanges between the two sides of the strait.... We are willing to hear opinions from people in Taiwan on the establishment of a mechanism for economic cooperation and the promotion of economic relations between the two sides.... The Democratic Progressive Party should think more about the welfare of the people in Taiwan, thoroughly discard its "Taiwan independence party platform," and develop cross-strait relations with a sincere attitude. We believe that the broad masses of the DPP

---

[172] President's interview on ABC's "Good Morning America" program, April 25, 2001; followed by interview on "CNN Inside Politics," April 25, 2001. The interviews took place one day after the annual arms sales talks with Taiwan authorities in Washington. Elaborating on the President's statements, Vice President Dick Cheney said that "the kind of diplomatic ambiguity people talk about may be OK in diplomacy sometimes. But when we get into an area where one side is displaying increasingly aggressive posture, if you will, toward the other, then it's appropriate to clarify here that in fact we're serious about this. It is an important step for the United States, and we don't want to see a misjudgment on the part of the Chinese" (interview on "Fox News Sunday," April 29, 2001).

[173] The adjustment in PRC policy came after Taiwan's elections on December 1, 2001, in which the DPP made significant gains in the legislature. The DPP won 87 seats, compared with the KMT's 68 seats, the People First Party (PFP)'s 46 seats, the Taiwan Solidarity Union (TSU)'s 13 seats, and the New Party's 1 seat. Independents make up the other 10 seats of the 225-seat Legislative Yuan. Also, the speech was given as the United States and the PRC prepared for President Bush's visit to Beijing on February 21-22, 2002.

[174] *People's Daily* (in Chinese and English) and *Xinhua* as translated by FBIS. The occasion for Vice Premier Qian Qichen's speech was the 7th anniversary of Jiang Zemin's "Eight Points." Also, the *People's Daily* published a related editorial on January 25, 2002.

are different from the minority of stubborn "Taiwan independence" elements. We welcome them to come, in appropriate capacities, to sightsee, visit, and increase their understanding.[175]

Bush-Jiang Press Conference in Beijing[176]

February 21, 2002

Jiang: *President Bush emphasized that the United States upholds the one China policy and will abide by the three Sino-U.S. joint communiques.*

Bush: *As [President Jiang] mentioned, we talked about Taiwan. The position of my government has not changed over the years. We believe in the peaceful settlement of this issue. We will urge there be no provocation. The United States will continue to support the Taiwan Relations Act.*

Taiwan President Chen on "One Country on Each Side"[177]

August 3, 2002

I would like to take a moment here to make a few calls for your consideration: (1) During these past few days, I have said that we must seriously consider going down Taiwan's own road.... What does "Taiwan's own road" mean? ... Taiwan's own road is Taiwan's road of democracy, Taiwan's road of freedom, Taiwan's road of human rights, and Taiwan's road of peace.

---

[175] While saying that its fundamental policy was unchanged, the PRC signaled a new receptive policy toward the ruling DPP and a change in tone (without reiterating the threat to use force). But, a week later, a spokesman for the PRC's Taiwan Affairs Office, Zhang Mingqing, excluded Chen Shui-bian and his vice president, Annette Lu, from the invitation to visit. While visiting Taiwan at about the same time, the Chairman and Managing Director of AIT, Richard Bush, spoke on January 28, 2002, saying that "it does not seem constructive for one side to set pre-conditions for a resumption of dialogue that the other side even suspects would be tantamount to conceding a fundamental issue before discussion begins."

[176] White House, "President Bush Meets with Chinese President Jiang Zemin," Great Hall of the People, Beijing, February 21, 2002. The visit to China was the President's second in four months, after the September 11, 2001 terrorist attacks. National Security Adviser Condoleezza Rice said that, in his meeting with Jiang, Bush restated the U.S. policy on Taiwan as a consistent policy and said that he hoped for a peaceful resolution and no provocations by either side, and that the United States will live up to the TRA. Bush also talked with students at Tsinghua University on February 22, and he explicitly mentioned the "one China policy" as one he has not changed. Nonetheless, Bush emphasized the U.S. defense commitment in the TRA and warned both Beijing and Taipei against provocations.

[177] Office of the President of the Republic of China, "Chen Shui-bian's Opening Address to the 29th Annual Meeting of the World Federation of Taiwanese Associations (in Tokyo, Japan) via Live Video Link," Chinese version (basis of the translation here) issued on August 3, and English version issued on August 7, 2002. Chen's remarks raised questions about whether he was changing policy to seek an independent Taiwan, whether there was coordination within his government, whether the speech would provoke tensions in the Taiwan Strait, and whether U.S. policy needed adjustment. On August 4, 2002, the NSC spokesman responded briefly that U.S. policy has not changed, and added on August 7, that "we have a one-China policy, and we do not support Taiwan independence" and that the United States "calls on all parties to avoid steps with might threaten cross-strait peace and stability, and urges a resumption of dialogue between Beijing and Taiwan." On August 8, the Chairwoman of Taiwan's Mainland Affairs Council, Tsai Ing-wen, visited Washington to tell the Administration and Congress that Taiwan's policy on cross-strait relations has not changed, remaining consistent with Chen's inauguration address. While in Beijing on August 26, 2002, Deputy Secretary of State Richard Armitage responded to a question about Chen's speech, saying that "the United States does not support Taiwan independence." He later explained that "by saying we do not support, it's one thing. It's different from saying we oppose it. If people on both sides of the strait came to an agreeable solution, then the United States obviously wouldn't inject ourselves. Hence, we use the term we don't 'support' it. But it's something to be resolved by the people on both sides of the question."

---

(2) Taiwan is our country, and our country cannot be bullied, diminished, marginalized, or downgraded as a local entity. Taiwan does not belong to someone else, nor is it someone else's local government or province. Taiwan also cannot become a second Hong Kong or Macau, because Taiwan is a sovereign independent country. Simply put, it must be clear that Taiwan and China are each one country on each side [yibian yiguo] of the strait.

(3) China has never renounced the use of force against Taiwan and continues to suppress Taiwan in the international community.... China's so-called "one China principle" or "one country, two systems" would change Taiwan's status quo. We cannot accept this, because whether Taiwan's future or status quo should be changed cannot be decided for us by any one country, any one government, any one political party, or any one person. Only the 23 million great people of Taiwan have the right to decide Taiwan's future, fate, and status. If the need arises, how should this decision be made? It is our long-sought ideal and goal, and our common idea: a referendum.... I sincerely call upon and encourage everyone to seriously consider the importance and urgency of legislation for holding referendums.

Bush-Jiang Summit in Crawford, Texas[178]

October 25, 2002

Bush: *On Taiwan, I emphasized to the President that our one China policy, based on the three communiques and the Taiwan Relations Act, remains unchanged. I stressed the need for dialogue between China and Taiwan that leads to a peaceful resolution of their differences.... The one China policy means that the issue ought to be resolved peacefully. We've got influence with some in the region; we intend to make sure that the issue is resolved peacefully and that includes making it clear that we do not support independence.*[179]

Jiang: *We have had a frank exchange of views on the Taiwan question, which is of concern to the Chinese side. I have elaborated my government's basic policy of peaceful unification and one country, two systems, for the settlement of the Taiwan question. President Bush has reiterated his clear-cut position, that the U.S. government abides by the one China policy.*[180]

---

[178] White House, "Remarks by the President and Chinese President Jiang Zemin in Press Conference," Bush Ranch, Crawford, TX, October 25, 2002. This summit was the third meeting between the two presidents.

[179] In contrast, PRC media reported that President Bush expressed to Jiang that the United States "opposes" (*fandui*) Taiwan independence. See "During Talks with Jiang Zemin, Bush Explicitly States for the First time 'Opposition to Taiwan Independence'," *Zhongguo Xinwen She*, October 26, 2002; *People's Daily* editorial (considered authoritative statement of PRC leadership views), "New Century, New Situation, New Actions," October 30, 2002. When asked about Bush's comments to Jiang, Assistant Secretary of State James Kelly maintained, at a November 19, 2002 press briefing, that "there has been no change in American policy and there was no change in the meeting or out of the meeting with respect to our position on Taiwan." Still, in a meeting with Rep. Henry Hyde, Chairman of the House International Relations Committee in Beijing on December 10, 2002, Jiang said he appreciated President Bush's "opposition" (*fandui* in Chinese version) to Taiwan independence, according to *People's Daily*. PRC experts on U.S.-China relations have reported since the meeting that Bush said that he was "against" Taiwan independence.

[180] As confirmed to Taiwan's legislature by its envoy to Washington, C.J. Chen, and reported in Taiwan's media (*Chung-Kuo Shih-Pao [China Times]*, November 22, 2002), President Jiang Zemin offered in vague terms a freeze or reduction in China's deployment of missiles targeted at Taiwan, in return for restraints in U.S. arms sales to Taiwan. President Bush reportedly did not respond to Jiang's linkage.

Bush's Meeting with PRC President Hu Jintao in France

June 1, 2003[181]

U.S.: *On Taiwan, the President repeated our policy of a one-China policy, based on the three communiques, the Taiwan Relations Act, no support for Taiwan independence. The Chinese basically accepted that, and said, okay, that's positive. They did say that they have concerns about forces on Taiwan moving towards independence. The President said, we don't support independence.*[182]

PRC: *President Hu reiterated China's principled stand on the Taiwan issue.... Bush said that the U.S. government will continue to follow the "one China" policy, abide by the three U.S.-China joint communiques, oppose "Taiwan independence," and that this policy has not changed and will not change.*[183]

President Chen Shui-bian on a New Constitution[184]

September 28, 2003[185]

If we consider the 1996 direct presidential election as the most significant symbol of Taiwan becoming a sovereign, democratic country, then, in 2006, this "complete" country will be 10 years old. Going through 10 years of practical experience, we must consider what we should seek next as a sovereign, democratic country. I must say that, in the next phase, we should further seek the deepening of democracy and a more efficient constitutional system, in order to lead Taiwan's people to face the rigorous challenges of the new century.[186]

---

[181] After the PRC blocked Taiwan's efforts to participate in the World Health Organization (WHO) in May 2003, despite the SARS epidemic, President Chen Shui-bian announced in a May 20, 2003 speech to the DPP, that he would promote a referendum on whether Taiwan should join the WHO. He called for that referendum and one on construction of a nuclear power plant to coincide with the presidential election in March 2004.

[182] In a background briefing released by the White House on June 1, 2003, an unnamed senior administration official volunteered to reporters this version of Bush's discussions on Taiwan in his first meeting with Hu Jintao after he became PRC president, in Evian, France.

[183] *People's Daily*, June 2, 2003. The official report in Chinese used *fandui* (oppose).

[184] On September 22-23, 2003, PRC Foreign Minister Li Zhaoxing visited Washington and met with President George Bush, Vice President Dick Cheney, National Security Advisor Condoleezza Rice, Secretary of State Colin Powell, and Secretary of Defense Donald Rumsfeld. Li reportedly complained about U.S. handling of the Taiwan issue.

[185] *Central News Agency*, Taipei, September 28, 2003; *Taipei Times*, September 29, 2003; *World Journal*, New York, September 30, 2003. Leading up to the next presidential election in March 2004, Chen Shui-bian announced a goal of enacting a new constitution for the people of Taiwan in time for the 20th anniversary of the founding of the DPP on September 28, 2006. Chen elaborated on his proposal in a speech on September 30, 2003, at a meeting of the Central Standing Committee of the DPP (translated from Chinese text). In response, on September 29, 2003, the State Department's spokesman called Chen's announcement an "individual campaign statement" and declined to take a position on Taiwan's domestic politics. Nonetheless, the U.S. response stressed "stability in the Taiwan Strait" and reminded Chen of his pledges in his inauguration speech of May 2000, saying that the United States "take them seriously and believe they should be adhered to."

[186] On November 11, 2003, Chen Shui-bian also issued a timetable: a new draft constitution by September 28, 2006; a referendum on the constitution on December 10, 2006; and enactment of the new constitution on May 20, 2008.

Bush's Meeting with Hu Jintao in Thailand[187]

October 19, 2003[188]

Bush: *President Hu and I have had a very constructive dialogue....*

Hu: *President Bush reiterated his government's position of adhering to the one China policy, the three China-U.S. joint communiques, and his opposition to Taiwan independence.*

Chen Shui-bian's Speech in New York[189]

October 31, 2003[190]

The hastening of a new Taiwan constitution will determine whether or not our democracy can come into full bloom. This, strengthened and supplemented by the institutions of direct democracy, such as referendums, will be a necessary step in advancing Taiwan's human rights and the deepening of its democracy. One must not be misled by the contention that holding referendums or re-engineering our constitutional framework bears any relevance to the "Five Noes" pledge presented in my inaugural speech. Neither should matters concerning Taiwan's constitutional development be simplistically interpreted as a political debate of unification versus independence.

---

[187] In briefing the press on President Bush's trip to Asia, National Security Advisor Condoleezza Rice said on October 14, 2003, that "nobody should try unilaterally to change the status quo... There must be a peaceful resolution of the cross-strait issue," in response to a question about Taiwan President Chen Shui-bian's statements regarding "one country on each side" of the Taiwan Strait.

[188] White House, "Remarks by President Bush and President Hu Jintao of China," Bangkok, Thailand, October 19, 2003. In making their joint public appearance, President Bush did not address the U.S. position on the Taiwan issue and did not correct President Hu's characterization of the U.S. position, including "opposition" to Taiwan independence. On October 20, 2003, *People's Daily* gave the PRC's official version of the meeting, reporting that Bush told Hu that the U.S. government upholds the one China policy, abides by the three communiques, and "opposes" (*fandui*) Taiwan independence, and that this policy will not change. An unnamed senior administration official briefed the press on the U.S. version of the meeting, according to a White House press release on October 19, 2003. When asked about Hu Jintao's characterization of Bush's "opposition" to Taiwan independence, the U.S. official said that U.S. policy on "one China" has not changed and that "we don't support Taiwan moving toward independence." When asked whether Hu Jintao misrepresented the U.S. view, the U.S. official replied, "I don't know" and reiterated Rice's message as one of not wanting either party to change the status quo unilaterally in the Taiwan Strait in a way that would upset peace and stability. "We're trying to make that clear," the official said.

[189] *Central News Agency*, Taipei, "Taiwan Never Slows Its Pace of Human Rights Reform: President," October 31, 2003. The United States allowed Chen Shui-bian to transit through New York on his way to Panama. While in New York, Chen received an award from the International League for Human Rights and gave this speech. At the Heritage Foundation, Deputy Assistant Secretary of State Randall Schriver told reporters that the Administration "appreciated" Chen's reiteration of his pledges in the inauguration speech of 2000 and that the transit "went very well." (*Central News Agency*, November 3, 2003). He also said that the Administration supported Chen's attendance at the "private event" and received an advance copy of Chen's speech "as a courtesy" (*Taipei Times*, November 5, 2003).

[190] On the same day, Chen Ming-tong, a vice chairman of Taiwan's Mainland Affairs Council (MAC), gave a speech at the 2nd World Convention of the Global Alliance for Democracy and Peace held in Houston, TX. He contended that Taiwan is already a sovereign, democratic country that is in a "post-independence period" and that the proposals for referendums and a new constitution are not meant to declare independence. He also said that Chen Shui-bian instructed Lee Yuan-tse, Taiwan's envoy to the APEC summit in Thailand in October 2003, to tell President Bush that the referendums have nothing to do with promoting Taiwan's independence.

U.S. "Opposition" to Change in Taiwan's Status[191]

December 1, 2003[192]

We oppose any attempt by either side to unilaterally change the status quo in the Taiwan Strait. We also urge both sides to refrain from actions or statements that increase tensions or make dialogue more difficult to achieve. Therefore, we would be opposed to any referenda that would change Taiwan's status or move toward independence. The United States has always held, and again reiterates, that cross-strait dialogue is essential to peace and stability in the Taiwan Strait area. President Chen pledged in his inaugural address in the year 2000 not to declare independence, not to change the name of Taiwan's government, and not to add the "state-to-state" theory to the constitution, and not to promote a referendum to change the status quo on independence or unification. We appreciate President Chen's pledge in 2000, and his subsequent reaffirmations of it, and we take it very seriously.

President Bush's Meeting with PRC Premier Wen Jiabao[193]

December 9, 2003

Bush [on whether Taiwan's President should cancel the referendum planned for March 20, 2004]: *The United States Government's policy is one China, based upon the three communiques and the Taiwan Relations Act. We oppose any unilateral decision by either China or Taiwan to change the status quo. And the comments and actions made by the leader of Taiwan indicate that he may be willing to make decisions unilaterally to change the status quo, which we oppose.*

Wen: *On many occasions, and just now in the meeting as well, President Bush has reiterated the U.S. commitment to the three Sino-U.S. Joint Communiques, the one China principle, and opposition to Taiwan independence. We appreciate that. In particular, we very much appreciate the position adopted by President Bush toward the latest moves and developments in Taiwan— that is, the attempt to resort to referendums of various kinds as an excuse to pursue Taiwan independence. We appreciate the position of the U.S. government.*

---

[191] On November 27, 2003, Taiwan's legislature passed legislation favored by the opposition parties (KMT and PFP) governing referendums while excluding a DPP proposal for referendums on the national name, flag, and other sovereignty issues. The law did authorize the president to hold a referendum on national security issues if Taiwan's sovereignty faced an external threat. President Chen then announced on November 29 that he would indeed hold a "defensive referendum" on the day of the election, on March 20, 2004.

[192] State Department Spokesman Richard Boucher, press briefing, December 1, 2003. National Security Advisor Condoleezza Rice stated on October 14, 2003, that "nobody should try unilaterally to change the status quo," but this was the first time the Bush Administration publicly stated "opposition" to any referendum that would change Taiwan's status. On the same day, the Senior Director of Asian Affairs at the National Security Council, James Moriarty, secretly met with President Chen in Taiwan and expressed U.S. concerns about "provocations," the *United Daily News* reported on December 1, 2003.

[193] White House, Remarks by President Bush and Premier Wen Jiabao in Photo Opportunity, the Oval Office, December 9, 2003. Bush did not make public remarks against the PRC's military threats toward Taiwan. On December 11, 2003, Representatives Brown, Chabot, Rohrabacher, and Wexler, the four co-Chairs of the Taiwan Caucus, wrote to President Bush, criticizing his remarks with Wen and urging him to support Taiwan's referendums. On March 17, 2004, 36 Members of the House, led by Representatives Peter Deutsch and Dana Rohrabacher, signed a letter to Taiwan's people in support of their right to hold referendums and to self-determination.

State Department's Testimony After Chen's Re-election[194]

April 21, 2004

The United States does not support independence for Taiwan or unilateral moves that would change the status quo as we define it. For Beijing, this means no use of force or threat to use force against Taiwan. For Taipei, it means exercising prudence in managing all aspects of cross-strait relations. For both sides, it means no statements or actions that would unilaterally alter Taiwan's status....

The President's message on December 9 of last year during PRC Premier Wen Jiabao's visit reiterated the U.S. Government's opposition to any unilateral moves by either China or Taiwan to change the status quo.... The United States will fulfill its obligations to help Taiwan defend itself, as mandated in the Taiwan Relations Act. At the same time, we have very real concerns that our efforts at deterring Chinese coercion might fail if Beijing ever becomes convinced Taiwan is embarked on a course toward independence and permanent separation from China, and concludes that Taiwan must be stopped in these efforts....

The United States strongly supports Taiwan's democracy, ... but we do not support Taiwan independence. A unilateral move toward independence will avail Taiwan of nothing it does not already enjoy in terms of democratic freedom, autonomy, prosperity, and security....

While strongly opposing the use of force by the PRC, we must also acknowledge with a sober mind what the PRC leaders have repeatedly conveyed about China's capabilities and intentions.... It would be irresponsible of us and of Taiwan's leaders to treat these statements as empty threats.... We encourage the people of Taiwan to regard this threat equally seriously. We look to President Chen to exercise the kind of responsible, democratic, and restrained leadership that will be necessary to ensure a peaceful and prosperous future for Taiwan....

As Taiwan proceeds with efforts to deepen democracy, we will speak clearly and bluntly if we feel as though those efforts carry the potential to adversely impact U.S. security interests or have the potential to undermine Taiwan's own security. There are limitations with respect to what the United States will support as Taiwan considers possible changes to its constitution....

Our position continues to be embodied in the so-called "Six Assurances" offered to Taiwan by President Reagan. We will neither seek to mediate between the PRC and Taiwan nor will we exert pressure on Taiwan to come to the bargaining table. Of course, the United States is also committed to make available defensive arms and defensive services to Taiwan in order to help Taiwan meet its self-defense needs. We believe a secure and self-confident Taiwan is a Taiwan that is more capable of engaging in political interaction and dialogue with the PRC, and we expect Taiwan will not interpret our support as a blank check to resist such dialogue....

War in the Strait would be a disaster for both sides and set them back decades, and undermine everything they and others in the region have worked so hard to achieve. We continue to urge Beijing and Taipei to pursue dialogue as soon as possible through any available channels, without preconditions....

---

[194] Testimony of Assistant Secretary of State for East Asian and Pacific Affairs James Kelly at hearing held by the House International Relations Committee on "The Taiwan Relations Act: The Next 25 Years," April 21, 2004.

The United States is committed to make available defensive arms and defensive services to Taiwan in order to help Taiwan meet its self-defense needs.... The PRC has explicitly committed itself publicly and in exchanges with the United States over the last 25 years to a fundamental policy "to strive for a peaceful resolution of the Taiwan question." If the PRC meets its obligations, and its words are matched by a military posture that bolsters and supports peaceful approaches to Taiwan, it follows logically that Taiwan's defense requirements will change....

Chen Shui-bian's Second Inaugural Address[195]

May 20, 2004[196]

The constitutional re-engineering project aims to enhance good governance and increase administrative efficiency, to ensure a solid foundation for democratic rule of law, and to foster long-term stability and prosperity of the nation.... By the time I complete my presidency in 2008, I hope to hand the people of Taiwan and to our country a new constitution[197]—one that is timely, relevant, and viable—as my historic responsibility and my commitment to the people. In the same context, I am fully aware that consensus has yet to be reached on issues related to national sovereignty, territory, and the subject of unification/independence; therefore, let me explicitly propose that these particular issues be excluded from the present constitutional re-engineering project. Procedurally, we shall follow the rules set out in the existing Constitution and its amendments....

If both sides are willing, on the basis of goodwill, to create an environment engendered upon "peaceful development and freedom of choice," then in the future, the Republic of China and the People's Republic of China—or Taiwan and China—can seek to establish relations in any form whatsoever. We would not exclude any possibility, so long as there is the consent of the 23 million people of Taiwan....

Today, I would like to reaffirm the promises and principles set forth in my inaugural speech in 2000. Those commitments have been honored. They have not changed over the past four years, nor will they change in the next four years....[198]

---

[195] Presidential Office of the Republic of China, "President Chen's Inaugural Address: Paving the Way for a Sustainable Taiwan," May 20, 2004, in Chinese with English version.

[196] On March 20, 2004, Chen Shui-bian of the DPP won re-election with 50.1 percent of the votes, while Lien Chan of the KMT received 49.9 percent. The opposition disputed the result of the election, in which Chen won with a margin of 0.2 percent, after surviving an assassination attempt the day before the election. The White House did not congratulate Chen Shui-bian on his victory until March 26, 2004, after official certification in Taiwan.

[197] While President Chen said "new constitution" in Chinese, the official English translation used "a new version of our constitution."

[198] The speech showed Chen Shui-bian responding positively to U.S. concerns after his re-election in March 2004 as to whether he would be pragmatic, predictable, and non-provocative. He did not repeat what Beijing perceives as antagonistic phrases such as "one country on each side" or "the status quo is Taiwan as an independent state." Chen did not rule out options for Taiwan's future. He also promised to seek constitutional changes using the process under the existing constitution and did not reiterate his call to use a referendum instead. Chen promised to exclude sovereignty issues from the constitutional changes. He reaffirmed the commitments in his inaugural address of 2000, while not explicitly re-stating the "Five Noes." The White House responded that the speech was "responsible and constructive" and presented another opportunity to restore cross-strait dialogue.

Colin Powell on Taiwan's Lack of Sovereignty[199]

October 25, 2004

There is only one China. Taiwan is not independent. It does not enjoy sovereignty as a nation, and that remains our policy, our firm policy. And it is a policy that has allowed Taiwan to develop a very vibrant democratic system, a market economic system, and provided great benefits to the people of Taiwan. And that is why we think it is a policy that should be respected and should remain in force and will remain in force, on the American side, it is our policy that clearly rests on the Three Communiques. To repeat it one more time: we do not support an independence movement in Taiwan.

Richard Armitage on the TRA and Mis-statement on Taiwan's Status[200]

December 10, 2004

We have the requirement with the Taiwan Relations Act to keep sufficient force in the Pacific to be able to deter attack; we are not required to defend. And these are questions that actually reside with the U.S. Congress, who has to declare an act of war. But I think we have to manage this question appropriately. We all agree that there is but one China, and Taiwan is part of China.

U.S.-Japan "2+2 Statement"[201]

February 19, 2005

[A common strategic objective is] "to encourage the peaceful resolution of issues concerning the Taiwan Strait through dialogue."

PRC's Hu Jintao on "Four-Point Guideline"[202]

March 4, 2005

1. Never sway in adhering to the one China principle.

2. Never give up efforts to seek peaceful reunification.

3. Never change the principle of placing hope on the Taiwan people.

---

[199] Secretary of State Colin Powell, Interview with Phoenix TV, Beijing, October 25, 2004.

[200] Deputy Secretary of State Richard Armitage, Interview with PBS, December 10, 2004. Armitage's note that "Taiwan is a part of China" was contrary to U.S. policy, which "acknowledged" the "one China" position of both sides. The TRA stipulates that Taiwan's status will be determined with a peaceful resolution. The State Department clarified at a news conference on December 22 that Armitage meant to simply re-state consistent U.S. policy.

[201] Secretary of Defense Donald Rumsfeld and Secretary of State Condoleezza Rice along with counterparts from Japan issued a Joint Statement of the U.S.-Japan Security Consultative Committee. China strongly objected to the alliance's mere mention of Taiwan.

[202] Right before adoption of the "Anti-Secession Law," Hu declared his "Four-Point Guidelines" before the Chinese People's Political Consultative Conference (CPPCC).

4. Never compromise in opposing "Taiwan independence" secessionist activities.

PRC's "Anti-Secession Law" of 2005[203]

March 14, 2005[204]

If the separatist forces of "Taiwan independence" use any name or any means to cause the fact of Taiwan's separation from China, or a major incident occurs that would lead to Taiwan's separation from China, or the possibilities of peaceful unification are completely exhausted, the country may adopt non-peaceful means and other necessary measures to safeguard national sovereignty and territorial integrity.

KMT-CPC Joint Statement of 2005 on "Peaceful Development"

April 29, 2005[205]

Hu Jintao and Lien Chan issued a joint press statement to summarize their agreement on goals: (1) resume cross-strait negotiation on the basis of the "1992 Consensus;" (2) cease hostilities, conclude a peace agreement, and launch military confidence building measures (CBMs); (3) comprehensively expand economic engagement; (4) negotiate Taiwan's international participation including in the WHO; (5) set up party-to-party platform.

Bush on U.S. Response to Provocations[206]

June 8, 2005

If China were to invade unilaterally, we would rise up in the spirit of the Taiwan Relations Act. If Taiwan were to declare independence unilaterally, it would be a unilateral decision, that would then change the U.S. equation, the U.S. look at what the ... the decision-making process. My attitude is, is that time will heal this issue. And therefore we're trying to make sure that neither side provokes the other through unilateral action.

---

[203] Translation of Article 8 of China's "Anti-Secession Law," adopted on March 14, 2005.

[204] At the February 15, 2005 hearing of the Senate Foreign Relations Committee on the nomination of Robert Zoellick to be Deputy Secretary of State, Zoellick responded to a question from Senator Lisa Murkowski on the Anti-Secession Law by publicly criticizing it as an action that would run counter to a peaceful resolution and dialogue. On March 16, the House passed (424-4) H.Con.Res. 98 (Hyde) to express grave concern about the "Anti-Secession Law," and the House Taiwan Caucus hosted a briefing by Taiwan's Ambassador David Lee. On April 6, 2005, the House International Relations Subcommittee on Asia and the Pacific held a hearing on China's "Anti-Secession Law."

[205] Despite the PRC's "Anti-Secession Law," KMT Chairman Lien Chan flew to Beijing for a historic meeting with CPC General-Secretary Hu Jintao. Some say, this first KMT-CPC meeting in 60 years began their 3rd United Front.

[206] George W. Bush, Interview with *Fox News*, June 8, 2005.

Chen Terminates the National Unification Guidelines[207]

February 27, 2006[208]

The National Unification Council will cease to function. No budget will be earmarked for it, and its personnel must return to their original posts. The National Unification Guidelines will cease to apply.

Bush-Hu Summit and "Peace and Stability"[209]

April 20, 2006

Bush: *We spent time talking about Taiwan, and I assured the President my position has not changed. I do not support independence for Taiwan.*

Hu: *During the meeting, I stressed the importance of the Taiwan question to Mr. President. Taiwan is an inalienable part of Chinese territory, and we maintain consistently that under the basis of the one China principle, we are committed to safeguard peace and stability in the Taiwan Strait, and to the promotion of the improvement and development of cross-strait relations.... We will by no means allow Taiwan independence. President Bush gave us his understanding of Chinese concerns. He reiterated the American positions and said that he does not hope that the moves taken by the Taiwan authorities to change the status quo will upset the China-U.S. relationship, which I am highly appreciative.*

State Department on a "Second Republic" in Taiwan[210]

October 17, 2006

The United States does not support Taiwan independence. We oppose unilateral changes to the status quo by either side.

---

[207] Despite his "Five Noes," on January 29, 2006, Chen Shui-bian called for consideration of whether to "abolish" the largely symbolic National Unification Council (NUC) and National Unification Guidelines (NUG). President Bush sent NSC official Dennis Wilder to Taipei with U.S. concerns. Representatives Dana Rohrabacher and Steve Chabot wrote a supportive commentary, "Principled Defense of Freedom," *Washington Times*, February 17, 2006. On February 27, Chen chaired a national security meeting and announced he would "terminate" (vs. "abolish") the NUC and NUG.

[208] Senator John Warner, Chairman of the Armed Services Committee, told Admiral William Fallon, Commander of the Pacific Command, at a committee hearing on March 7, 2006, that "if conflict were precipitated by just inappropriate and wrongful politics generated by the Taiwanese elected officials, I'm not entirely sure that this nation would come full force to their rescue if they created that problem."

[209] White House, "President Bush Meets with President Hu of the People's Republic of China," Oval Office, April 20, 2006.

[210] State Department, question taken at the press briefing, October 17, 2006. On October 15, President Chen Shui-bian called for consideration of a proposal for a "second republic" made by former presidential advisor Koo Kwang-ming. Later, Chen elaborated on the concept of a constitution for a "second republic" by saying: "The current constitution would be frozen, and a new Taiwan constitution would be written. Freezing the [Republic of China] constitution also means keeping some kind of a link to the [old] ROC constitution and not cutting if off completely. The preamble to a new constitution could address the territory of Taiwan, but the relevant sections of the old constitution defining the territory would not be touched, thus avoiding a change to the status quo." (Interview with Kathrin Hille, "Taiwan Set for New Clash With Beijing," *Financial Times*, November 1, 2006). Shortly before he became Chairman of the Mainland Affairs Commission, Chen Ming-tong released such a draft constitution on March 18, 2007.

State Department on "Name Rectification" in Taiwan[211]

February 9, 2007[212]

We do not support administrative steps by the Taiwan authorities that would appear to change Taiwan's status unilaterally or move toward independence. The United States does not, for instance, support changes in terminology for entities administered by the Taiwan authorities. President Chen's fulfillment of his commitments will be a test of leadership, dependability, and statesmanship, as well as ability to protect Taiwan's interests, its relations with others, and to maintain peace and stability in the Strait.

U.S. Opposition to Taiwan's Referendum on Joining U.N.

June 19, 2007[213]

The United States opposes any initiative that appears designed to change Taiwan's status unilaterally. This would include a referendum on whether to apply to the United Nations under the name Taiwan. While such a referendum would have no practical impact on Taiwan's U.N. status, it would increase tensions in the Taiwan Strait. Maintenance of peace and stability across the Taiwan Strait is of vital interest to the people of Taiwan and serves U.S. security interests as well. Moreover, such a move would appear to run counter to President Chen's repeated commitments to President Bush and the international community. We urge President Chen to exercise leadership by rejecting such a proposed referendum.

---

[211] State Department, question taken at the press briefing, February 9, 2007. On February 8, President Chen Shui-bian supported DPP Chairman Yu Shyi-kun's proposal to promote a "name rectification" campaign, by renaming three state-owned entities: China Petroleum Corporation to CPC Corporation Taiwan; China Shipbuilding Corporation to CSBC Corporation Taiwan; and Chunghwa Postal Company" to "Taiwan Postal Company." But people in Taiwan at the time did not voice major concern about the changes in name.

[212] On February 20, 2007, Representative Tom Tancredo wrote a letter to Secretary of State Condoleezza Rice to criticize her department's rebuke of Chen over "trivial things" and to question how changing the names of local businesses would change Taiwan's status. On April 24, 2007, at a hearing of the Senate Armed Services Committee, Senator John Warner said to the Pacific Command's commander, Admiral Timothy Keating, that the U.S. military is heavily engaged worldwide and that Taiwan should not play the "TRA card."

[213] State Department, daily press briefing, June 19, 2007. On June 18, President Chen Shui-bian called for a referendum on whether to join the U.N. using the name "Taiwan" to be held at the time of the presidential election in March 2008. Chen contended that Taiwan long participated in various international gatherings using different designations. Representative Tom Lantos, Chairman of the House Foreign Affairs Committee, met with Taiwan's Vice President Annette Lu during her transit in San Francisco on July 2, 2007, and said in an interview that it is impractical for Taiwan to seek membership in the U.N. and that neither the Bush Administration nor Congress supported a referendum on Taiwan's membership in the U.N. (*Central News Agency*, July 4, 2007). Later, Representative Tom Tancredo wrote a letter on August 30, 2007, to Secretary of State Condoleezza Rice to criticize Deputy Secretary of State John Negroponte's comments opposing the referendum as "a step towards a declaration of independence of Taiwan" (in interview by pro-PRC *Phoenix TV* of Hong Kong on August 27, 2007). On September 6, PRC ruler Hu Jintao told President Bush in Sydney, Australia, that the situation in Taiwan entered a "highly dangerous period." Deputy Assistant Secretary of State Thomas Christensen followed with a strongly-worded speech on September 11, that stressed U.S. opposition to this referendum as "an apparent pursuit of name change." On September 30, the DPP passed a "Resolution on a Normal Country." On December 6, Christensen criticized the referendum as intended to pursue a "unilateral change in the status quo." On December 19, Representatives Tom Tancredo and Dana Rohrabacher wrote a letter to Secretary of State Rice asking her department to "cease its repeated efforts to affect the outcome of the upcoming elections in Taiwan, and specifically, the outcome of the planned referendum on membership in the United Nations." But at a press conference two days later, Rice attacked the referendum as "provocative."

U.S. Non-Support for "Taiwan's" Membership in the U.N.

September 21, 2007[214]

The United States supports Taiwan's meaningful participation in international organizations whenever appropriate. Such involvement is in the interest of the 23 million people of Taiwan and the international community, and we urge all UN members to set aside preconditions and work creatively toward this goal. Consistent with our long-standing One China policy, the United States does not support Taiwan's membership in international organizations where statehood is a requirement, so it cannot support measures designed to advance that goal. We believe that efforts to urge UN membership for Taiwan will detract from our goal of advancing Taiwan's involvement in international society.

KMT President Ma Ying-jeou's Inaugural Address and "3 Noes"

May 20, 2008[215]

I sincerely hope that the two sides of the Taiwan Strait can seize this historic opportunity to achieve peace and co-prosperity. Under the principle of "no unification, no independence, and no use of force," as Taiwan's mainstream public opinion holds it, and under the framework of the ROC Constitution, we will maintain the status quo in the Taiwan Strait. In 1992, the two sides reached a consensus on "one China, respective interpretations." Many rounds of negotiation were then completed, spurring the development of cross-strait relations. I want to reiterate that, based on the "1992 Consensus," negotiations should resume at the earliest time possible.... We will also enter consultatons with mainland China over Taiwan's international space and a possible cross-strait peace accord.... In resolving cross-strait issues, what matters is not sovereignty but core values and way of life.

---

[214] Departing from previous applications since 1993 to join the U.N. under the formal name of Republic of China, President Chen Shui-bian wrote letters in July 2007 to apply for membership for "Taiwan." At a press conference at the White House on August 30, 2007, NSC official Dennis Wilder said that "membership in the United Nations requires statehood. Taiwan, or the Republic of China, is not at this point a state in the international community." The United States did not agree with Taiwan or with the PRC, which claimed that **U.N. Resolution 2758** of October 25, 1971, recognized Taiwan as a part of China. The PRC's interpretation was used by U.N. Secretary-General Ban Ki-moon of South Korea. In fact, that resolution restored the legal rights of the PRC in the U.N. and expelled "the representatives of Chiang Kai-shek" but did not address the status of or mention Taiwan. Three of the co-chairs of the House Taiwan Caucus wrote to criticize Ban's "diplomatic error" and to urge U.S. support for "Taiwan's right to apply for a meaningful U.N. role" (Representatives Steve Chabot, Shelley Berkley, and Dana Rohrabacher, "Don't Abandon Taiwan," *Washington Times*, September 17, 2007). While the State Department did not speak at the General Assembly on Taiwan's application to join the U.N., the U.S. Mission to the U.N. issued a statement on September 21, 2007.

[215] For Taiwan's second democratic turnover of power, the KMT's Ma Ying-jeou won the presidential election on March 22, 2008, with a surprising, solid margin of victory (by 17% points; 2.2 million votes), against DPP candidate Frank Hsieh. Ma won 58.5% of the votes, while Hsieh won 41.5%. The KMT and DPP referendums on membership in the U.N., targets of U.S. and PRC condemnation, failed to become valid after only 36% of voters participated in both referendums (50% participation was required for validity). On author's observation at the election, see CRS Report RL34441, *Security Implications of Taiwan's Presidential Election of March 2008*, by Shirley A. Kan.

PRC Leader Hu Jintao on "Peaceful Development"

December 31, 2008[216]

Hu Jintao made six proposals: (1) Abide by the "one China" principle and enhance political mutual trust; (2) advance economic cooperation and common development; (3) promote Chinese culture and strengthen the spiritual bond; (4) strengthen people-to-people exchanges, with the DPP putting an end to "Taiwan independence" separatist activities; (5) safeguard national sovereignty and consult on foreign affairs, including Taiwan's participation in the activities of international organizations; (6) end the state of hostility and reach a peace agreement, including exploring the establishment of a mechanism of mutual trust for military security.

Statements During Obama Administration

President Obama Reiterated "One China" Policy, including TRA

November 17, 2009

We also applauded the steps that the People's Republic of China and Taiwan have already taken to relax tensions and build ties across the Taiwan Strait. Our own policy, based on the three U.S.-China communiqués and the Taiwan Relations Act, supports the further development of these ties—ties that are in the interest of both sides, as well as the broader region and the United States.[217]

U.S.-PRC Joint Statement of 2009 on "Peaceful Development"

November 17, 2009

The United States and China underscored the importance of the Taiwan issue in U.S.-China relations. China emphasized that the Taiwan issue concerns China's sovereignty and territorial integrity, and expressed the hope that the United States will honor its relevant commitments and appreciate and support the Chinese's side position on this issue. The United States stated that it follows its One China policy and abides by the principles of the three U.S.-China Joint Communiques. The United States welcomes the peaceful development of relations across the Taiwan Strait and looks forward to efforts by both sides to increase dialogues and interactions in economic, political, and other fields, and develop more positive and stable cross-strait relations.[218]

---

[216] Responding to Ma Ying-jeou's overtures, Hu Jintao apparently authorized potential cross-strait military negotiations that could include confidence building measures (CBMs), a goal also raised in the CPC-KMT statement of 2005.

[217] White House, "Joint Press Statement by President Obama and President Hu of China," Beijing, November 17, 2009. The two leaders issued statements rather than offer a news conference during their summit. President Obama reiterated his commitment to the TRA and continuity in policy, but the day before, he neglected to include the TRA as part of U.S. policy on Taiwan. At a town hall in Shanghai on November 16, President Obama answered a question on arms sales to Taiwan by saying that "I have been clear in the past that my administration fully supports a one China policy, as reflected in the three joint communiqués that date back several decades, in terms of our relations with Taiwan as well as our relations with the People's Republic of China. We don't want to change that policy and that approach."

[218] White House, "U.S.-China Joint Statement," November 17, 2009, issued during Obama's summit with Hu Jintao in Beijing as the first such joint statement in 12 years. After that paragraph on Taiwan, a question arose about whether the (continued...)

Ma Ying-jeou on Never Asking for U.S. Defense of Taiwan

April 30, 2010

We will continue to reduce the risks so that we will purchase arms from the United States, but we will never ask the Americans to fight for Taiwan.[219]

Robert Gates on Arms Sales and "Opposition" to Taiwan's Independence

June 2010

From the time of normalization on, the United States, as a result of the Taiwan Relations Act of 1979, has been obligated to provide minimal levels of defensive capability for Taiwan. Having been through this in 2007 with the Bush administration and last year with the Obama administration, I can tell you that in both administrations the items that were considered for sale were carefully thought-through with a focus on ensuring that we were providing defensive capabilities and, at the same time, underscoring, as I said in my remarks, our continued opposition to independence for Taiwan.[220]

(...continued)

next one applied to Taiwan: "The two countries reiterated that the fundamental principle of respect for each other's sovereignty and territorial integrity is at the core of the three U.S.-China Joint Communiques which guide U.S.-China relations. Neither side supports any attempts by any force to undermine this principle. The two sides agreed that respecting each other's *core interests* [emphasis added] is extremely important to ensure steady progress in U.S.-China relations." However, AIT Chairman Ray Burghardt clarified at a news conference in Taipei on November 24, 2009, that in the negotiating history of the Joint Statement, only one paragraph was relevant to Taiwan, while the next paragraph on "core interests" was negotiated to cover Tibet and Xinjiang. Burghardt also stated that the Joint Statement should not be interpreted as putting pressure on Taiwan to negotiate with the PRC. He concluded that the TRA remained "the core document that guides relations between the people of the United States and Taiwan."

[219] President Ma's interview with *CNN*, published on May 1, 2010; author's consultation, Taipei, June 2010. In addition, Ma reiterated this stance in an attempt to assure visiting Senator Dianne Feinstein the next month.

[220] Defense Department, "Remarks by Secretary Gates at the Shangri-La Dialogue, International Institute for Strategic Studies," Singapore, June 4, 2010. Contrary to U.S. policy, Gates repeated this "opposition" to Taiwan's independence in testimony at a hearing of the Senate Appropriations Committee on June 16, 2010.

U.S.-PRC Joint Statement of 2011

January 19, 2011[221]

Both sides underscored the importance of the Taiwan issue in U.S.-China relations. The Chinese side emphasized that the Taiwan issue concerns China's sovereignty and territorial integrity, and expressed the hope that the U.S. side will honor its relevant commitments and appreciate and support the Chinese side's position on this issue. The U.S. side stated that the United States follows its one China policy and abides by the principles of the three U.S.-China Joint Communiqués. The United States applauded the Economic Cooperation Framework Agreement between the two sides of the Taiwan Strait and welcomed the new lines of communications developing between them. The United States supports the peaceful development of relations across the Taiwan Strait and looks forward to efforts by both sides to increase dialogues and interactions in economic, political, and other fields, and to develop more positive and stable cross-Strait relations.

Note: This study was originally prepared at the request of Senate Majority Leader Trent Lott in the 106th Congress and is made available for general congressional use with permission.

Author Contact Information

Shirley A. Kan
Specialist in Asian Security Affairs
skan@crs.loc.gov, 7-7606

---

[221] Presidents Obama and Hu issued their second U.S.-PRC Joint Statement, during Hu's state visit in Washington. While a joint statement would not refer to the TRA, Secretary of State Hillary Clinton delivered a speech five days prior that explicitly stated U.S. policy as guided by the three Joint Communiqués as well as the TRA and added a call for China to reduce military tension and deployments affecting Taiwan. President Obama cited the TRA in his remarks at the joint press conference. On January 25, AIT Chairman Ray Burghardt visited Taipei and discussed Hu's visit and the Joint Statement with President Ma Ying-jeou. President Ma noted that U.S. policy has been consistent with the TRA as well as the Six Assurances. In his press conference, Burghardt also reaffirmed aspects of the Six Assurances, assured that the United States was mindful of Taiwan, and clarified that the United States did not agree to issue the statement if China insisted on calling it another "communique" or including "core interests." In contrast to the Joint Statement of 2009, this Joint Statement did not repeat a reference to China's "core interests." The Joint Statement of 2011 added a new reference to the cross-strait Economic Cooperation Framework Agreement (ECFA) of 2010, which was pushed by the ruling KMT and President Ma but criticized by the opposition DPP. (PRC State Councilor Dai Bingguo issued an article in December 2010 that re-affirmed China's "core interests" as leadership of the Communist Party of China (CPC); sovereignty and territorial integrity; and economic and social development.)

www.ingramcontent.com/pod-product-compliance
Lightning Source LLC
Chambersburg PA
CBHW080322290526
45790CB00005B/2144